Predictive Analytics with Microsoft Azure Machine Learning

Build and Deploy Actionable Solutions in Minutes

Roger Barga

Valentine Fontama

Wee Hyong Tok

Predictive Analytics with Microsoft Azure Machine Learning: Build and Deploy Actionable Solutions in Minutes

ISBN-13 (pbk): 978-1-4842-0446-7

ISBN-13 (electronic): 978-1-4842-0445-0

Managing Director: Welmoed Spahr
Lead Editor: James DeWolf
Development Editor: Douglas Pundick
Technical Reviewers: Jacob Spoelstra and Hang Zhang
Editorial Board: Steve Anglin, Mark Beckner, Gary Cornell, Louise Corrigan, James DeWolf,
    Jonathan Gennick, Robert Hutchinson, Michelle Lowman, James Markham,
    Matthew Moodie, Jeff Olson, Jeffrey Pepper, Douglas Pundick, Ben Renow-Clarke,
    Dominic Shakeshaft, Gwenan Spearing, Matt Wade, Steve Weiss
Coordinating Editor: Kevin Walter
Copy Editor: Mary Behr
Compositor: SPi Global
Indexer: SPi Global
Artist: SPi Global
Cover Designer: Anna Ishchenko

Distributed to the book trade worldwide by Springer Science+Business Media New York, 233 Spring Street, 6th Floor, New York, NY 10013. Phone 1-800-SPRINGER, fax (201) 348-4505, e-mail orders-ny@springer-sbm.com, or visit www.springeronline.com. Apress Media, LLC is a California LLC and the sole member (owner) is Springer Science + Business Media Finance Inc (SSBM Finance Inc). SSBM Finance Inc is a **Delaware** corporation.

For information on translations, please e-mail rights@apress.com, or visit www.apress.com.

Apress and friends of ED books may be purchased in bulk for academic, corporate, or promotional use. eBook versions and licenses are also available for most titles. For more information, reference our Special Bulk Sales–eBook Licensing web page at www.apress.com/bulk-sales.

Any source code or other supplementary materials referenced by the author in this text is available to readers at www.apress.com. For detailed information about how to locate your book's source code, go to www.apress.com/source-code/.

Contents at a Glance

About the Authors.. xi

Acknowledgments xiii

Foreword xv

Introduction xix

■Part 1: Introducing Data Science and Microsoft Azure
Machine Learning 1

■Chapter 1: Introduction to Data Science............................. 3

■Chapter 2: Introducing Microsoft Azure Machine Learning.......... 21

■Chapter 3: Integration with R 43

■Part 2: Statistical and Machine Learning Algorithms... 65

■Chapter 4: Introduction to Statistical and Machine
Learning Algorithms 67

■Part 3: Practical Applications.. 85

■Chapter 5: Building Customer Propensity Models....................... 87

■Chapter 6: Building Churn Models..................................... 107

■Chapter 7: Customer Segmentation Models 129

■Chapter 8: Building Predictive Maintenance Models................. 143

Index.. 163

Contents

About the Authors... xi

Acknowledgments xiii

Foreword xv

Introduction xix

■Part 1: Introducing Data Science and Microsoft Azure
   Machine Learning 1

■Chapter 1: Introduction to Data Science...................................... 3

What Is Data Science? 3

Analytics Spectrum 4

    Descriptive Analysis...5

    Diagnostic Analysis...5

    Predictive Analysis..5

    Prescriptive Analysis 6

Why Does It Matter and Why Now? 7

    Data as a Competitive Asset..7

    Increased Customer Demand 8

    Increased Awareness of Data Mining Technologies...............................8

    Access to More Data..8

    Faster and Cheaper Processing Power...9

    The Data Science Process 11

Common Data Science Techniques 14

    Classification Algorithms 14

    Clustering Algorithms 15

    Regression Algorithms.. 16

    Simulation 17

    Content Analysis 17

    Recommendation Engines... 18

Cutting Edge of Data Science.. 18

    The Rise of Ensemble Models 18

Summary.. 20

Bibliography 20

▓Chapter 2: Introducing Microsoft Azure Machine Learning.......... 21

Hello, Machine Learning Studio! 21

Components of an Experiment... 22

Five Easy Steps to Creating an Experiment....................................... 23

    Step 1: Get Data... 24

    Step 2: Preprocess Data 26

    Step 3: Define Features 29

    Step 4: Choose and Apply Machine Learning Algorithms 31

    Step 5: Predict Over New Data 33

Deploying Your Model in Production... 35

    Deploying Your Model into Staging..................................... 36

    Testing the Web Service 39

    Moving Your Model from Staging into Production 39

    Accessing the Azure Machine Learning Web Service.............. 40

Summary.. 42

▓Chapter 3: Integration with R 43

R in a Nutshell 43

Building and Deploying Your First R Script 45

Using R for Data Preprocessing 50

Using a Script Bundle (Zip) 54

Building and Deploying a Decision Tree Using R 58

Summary 64

▓Part 2: Statistical and Machine Learning Algorithms... 65

▓Chapter 4: Introduction to Statistical and Machine Learning Algorithms 67

Regression Algorithms 67

    Linear Regression 68

    Neural Networks 70

    Decision Trees 72

    Boosted Decision Trees 73

Classification Algorithms 74

    Support Vector Machines 76

    Bayes Point Machines 78

Clustering Algorithms 79

Summary 83

▓Part 3: Practical Applications 85

▓Chapter 5: Building Customer Propensity Models 87

The Business Problem 87

Data Acquisition and Preparation 88

    Loading Data from Your Local File System 88

    Loading Data from Other Sources 89

    Data Analysis 91

Training the Model.. 99

Model Testing and Validation.. 101

Model Performance 102

Summary... 106

▓Chapter 6: Building Churn Models... 107

Churn Models in a Nutshell 107

Building and Deploying a Customer Churn Model................. 109

    Preparing and Understanding Data 109

    Data Preprocessing and Feature Selection 114

    Classification Model for Predicting Churn 121

    Evaluating the Performance of the Customer Churn Models.................... 125

Summary... 127

▓Chapter 7: Customer Segmentation Models 129

Customer Segmentation Models in a Nutshell 129

Building and Deploying Your First K-Means Clustering Model 130

    Feature Hashing 133

    Identifying the Right Features 134

    Properties of K-Means Clustering.. 136

Customer Segmentation of Wholesale Customers 138

    Loading the Data from the UCI Machine Learning Repository................. 138

    Using K-Means Clustering for Wholesale Customer Segmentation.......... 139

    Cluster Assignment for New Data.. 141

Summary... 142

▓Chapter 8: Building Predictive Maintenance Models.................. 143

Overview 143

The Business Problem.. 145

Data Acquisition and Preparation 145

The Dataset 145

Data Loading... 146

Data Analysis 149

Training the Model... 152

Model Testing and Validation... 164

Model Performance 155

Model Deployment 158

Publishing Your Model into Staging 158

Moving Your Model from Staging into Production 160

Summary.. 161

Index... 163

About the Authors

Roger Barga is a General Manager and Director of Development at Amazon Web Services. Prior to joining Amazon, Roger was Group Program Manager for the Cloud Machine Learning group in the Cloud & Enterprise division at Microsoft, where his team was responsible for product management of the Azure Machine Learning service. Roger joined Microsoft in 1997 as a Researcher in the Database Group of Microsoft Research, where he directed both systems research and product development efforts in database, workflow, and stream processing systems. He has developed ideas from basic research, through proof of concept prototypes, to incubation efforts in product groups. Prior to joining Microsoft, Roger was a Research Scientist in the Machine Learning Group at the Pacific Northwest National Laboratory where he built and deployed machine learning-based solutions. Roger is also an Affiliate Professor at the University of Washington, where he is a lecturer in the Data Science and Machine Learning programs.

Roger holds a PhD in Computer Science, a M.Sc. in Computer Science with an emphasis on Machine Learning, and a B.Sc. in Mathematics and Computing Science. He has published over 90 peer-reviewed technical papers and book chapters, collaborated with 214 co-authors from 1991 to 2013, with over 700 citations by 1,084 authors.

Valentine Fontama is a Principal Data Scientist in the Data and Decision Sciences Group (DDSG) at Microsoft, where he leads external consulting engagements that deliver world-class Advanced Analytics solutions to Microsoft's customers. Val has over 18 years of experience in data science and business. Following a PhD in Artificial Neural Networks, he applied data mining in the environmental science and credit industries. Before Microsoft, Val was a New Technology Consultant at Equifax in London where he pioneered the application of data mining to risk assessment and marketing in the consumer credit industry. He is currently an Affiliate Professor of Data Science at the University of Washington.

In his prior role at Microsoft, Val was a Senior Product Marketing Manager responsible for big data and predictive analytics in cloud and enterprise marketing. In this role, he led product management for Microsoft Azure Machine Learning; HDInsight, the first

Hadoop service from Microsoft; Parallel Data Warehouse, Microsoft's first data warehouse appliance; and three releases of Fast Track Data Warehouse. He also played a key role in defining Microsoft's strategy and positioning for in-memory computing.

Val holds an M.B.A. in Strategic Management and Marketing from Wharton Business School, a Ph.D. in Neural Networks, a M.Sc. in Computing, and a B.Sc. in Mathematics and Electronics (with First Class Honors). He co-authored the book *Introducing Microsoft Azure HDInsight*, and has published 11 academic papers with 152 citations by over 227 authors.

 **Wee-Hyong Tok** is a Senior Program Manager on the SQL Server team at Microsoft. Wee-Hyong brings over 12 years of database systems experience (with more than six years of data platform experience in industry and six years of academic experience).

Prior to pursuing his PhD, Wee-Hyong was a System Analyst at a large telecommunication company in Singapore, working on marketing decision support systems. Following his PhD in Data Streaming Systems from the National University of Singapore, he joined Microsoft and worked on the SQL Server team. Over the past six years, Wee-Hyong gained extensive experience working with distributed engineering teams from Asia and US, and was responsible for shaping the SSIS Server, bringing it from concept to release in SQL Server 2012. More recently, Wee-Hyong was part of the Azure Data Factory team, a service for orchestrating and managing data transformation and movement.

Wee Hyong holds a Ph.D. in Data Streaming Systems, a M.Sc. in Computing, and a B.Sc. (First Class Honors) in Computer Science, from the National University of Singapore. He has published 21 peer reviewed academic papers and journals. He is a co-author of two books, *Introducing Microsoft Azure HDInsight* and *Microsoft SQL Server 2012 Integration Services*.

Acknowledgments

I would like to express my gratitude to the many people in the CloudML team at Microsoft who saw us through this book; to all those who provided support, read, offered comments, and assisted in the editing, and proofreading. I wish to thank my coauthors, Val and Wee-Hyong, for their drive and perseverance which was key to completing this book, and to our publisher Apress, especially Kevin Walter and James T. DeWolf, for making this all possible. Above all I want to thank my wife, Terre, and my daughters Amelie and Jolie, who supported and encouraged me in spite of all the time it took me away from them.

—Roger Barga

I would like to thank my co-authors, Roger and Wee-Hyong, for their deep collaboration on this project. Special thanks to my wife, Veronica, and loving kids, Engu, Chembe, and Nayah, for their support and encouragement.

—Valentine Fontama

I would like to thank my coauthors, Roger and Val, for working together to shape the content of the book. I deeply appreciate the reviews by the team of data scientists from the CLoudML team. I'd also like to thank the Apress team who worked with us from concept to shipping. And I'd like to thank Juliet, Nathaniel, Siak-Eng, and Hwee-Tiang for their love, support, and patience.

—Wee-Hyong

Foreword

Few people appreciate the enormous potential of machine learning (ML) in enterprise applications. I was lucky enough to get a taste of its potential benefits just a few months into my first job. It was 1995 and credit card issuers were beginning to adopt neural network models to detect credit card fraud in real time. When a credit card is used, transaction data from the point of sale system is sent to the card issuer's credit authorization system where a neural network scores for the probability of fraud. If the probability is high, the transaction is declined in real time. I was a scientist building such models and one of my first model deliveries was for a South American bank. When the model was deployed, the bank identified over a million dollars of previously undetected fraud on the very first day. This was a big eye-opener. In the years since, I have seen ML deliver huge value in diverse applications such as demand forecasting, failure and anomaly detection, ad targeting, online recommendations, and virtual assistants like Cortana. By embedding ML into their enterprise systems, organizations can improve customer experience, reduce the risk of systemic failures, grow revenue, and realize significant cost savings.

However, building ML systems is slow, time-consuming, and error prone. Even though we are able to analyze very large data sets these days and deploy at very high transaction rates, the following bottlenecks remain:

- ML system development requires deep expertise. Even though the core principles of ML are now accessible to a wider audience, talented data scientists are as hard to hire today as they were two decades ago.

- Practitioners are forced to use a variety of tools to collect, clean, merge, and analyze data. These tools have a steep learning curve and are not integrated. Commercial ML software is expensive to deploy and maintain.

- Building and verifying models requires considerable experimentation. Data scientists often find themselves limited by compute and storage because they need to run a large number of experiments that generate considerable new data.

- Software tools do not support scalable experimentation or methods for organizing experiment runs. The act of collaborating with a team on experiments and sharing derived variables, scripts, etc. is manual and ad-hoc without tools support. Evaluating and debugging statistical models remains a challenge.

Data scientists work around these limitations by writing custom programs and by doing undifferentiated heavy lifting as they perform their ML experiments. But it gets harder in the deployment phase. Deploying ML models in a mission-critical business process such as real-time fraud prevention or ad targeting requires sophisticated engineering. The following needs must be met:

- Typically, ML models that have been developed offline now have to be reimplemented in a language such as C++, C#, or Java.

- The transaction data pipelines have to be plumbed. Data transformations and variables used in the offline models have to be recoded and compiled.

- These reimplementations inevitably introduce bugs, requiring verification that the models work as originally designed.

- A custom container for the model has to be built, with appropriate monitors, metrics, and logging.

- Advanced deployments require A/B testing frameworks to evaluate alternative models side-by-side. One needs mechanisms to switch models in or out, preferably without recompiling and deploying the entire application.

- One has to validate that the candidate production model works as originally designed through statistical tests.

The automated decisions made by the system and the business outcomes have to be logged for refining the ML models and for monitoring.

The service has to be designed for high availability, disaster recovery, and geo-proximity to end points.

When the service has to be scaled to meet higher transaction rates and/or low latency, more work is required to provision new hardware, deploy the service to new machines, and scale out.

All of these are time-consuming and engineering-intensive steps, expensive in terms of both infrastructure and manpower. The end-to-end engineering and maintenance of a production ML application requires a highly skilled team that few organizations can build and sustain.

Microsoft Azure ML was designed to solve these problems.

- It's a fully managed cloud service with no software to install, no hardware to manage, no OS versions or development environments to grapple with.

- Armed with nothing but a browser, data scientists can log on to Azure and start developing ML models from any location, from any device. They can host a practically unlimited number of files on Azure storage.

- ML Studio, an integrated development environment for ML, lets you set up experiments as simple data flow graphs, with an easy-to-use drag, drop, and connect paradigm. Data scientists can avoid programming for a large number of common tasks, allowing them to focus on experiment design and iteration.

- Many sample experiments are provided to make it easy to get started.

- A collection of best of breed algorithms developed by Microsoft Research is built in, as is support for custom R code. Over 350 open source R packages can be used securely within Azure ML.

- Data flow graphs can have several parallel paths that automatically run in parallel, allowing scientists to execute complex experiments and make side by-side comparisons without the usual computational constraints.

- Experiments are readily sharable, so others can pick up on your work and continue where you left off.

Azure ML also makes it simple to create production deployments at scale in the cloud. Pre-trained ML models can be incorporated into a scoring workflow and, with a few clicks, a new cloud-hosted REST API can be created. This REST API has been engineered to respond with low latency. No reimplementation or porting is required–a key benefit over traditional data analytics software. Data from anywhere on the Internet (laptops, web sites, mobile devices, wearables, and connected machines) can be sent to the newly created API to get back predictions. For example, a data scientist can create a fraud detection API that takes transaction information as input and returns a low/medium/high risk indicator as output. Such an API would then be "live" on the cloud, ready to accept calls from any software that a developer chooses to call it from. The API backend scales elastically, so that when transaction rates spike, the Azure ML service can automatically handle the load. There are virtually no limits on the number of ML APIs that a data scientist can create and deploy–and all this without any dependency on engineering. For engineering and IT, it becomes simple to integrate a new ML model using those REST APIs, and testing multiple models side-by-side before deployment becomes easy, allowing dramatically better agility at low cost. Azure provides mechanisms to scale and manage APIs in production, including mechanisms to measure availability, latency, and performance. Building robust, highly available, reliable ML systems and managing the production deployment is therefore dramatically faster, cheaper, and easier for the enterprise, with huge business benefits.

We believe Azure ML is a game changer. It makes the incredible potential of ML accessible both to startups and large enterprises. Startups are now able to use the same capabilities that were previously available to only the most sophisticated businesses. Larger enterprises are able to unleash the latent value in their big data to generate significantly more revenue and efficiencies. Above all, the speed of iteration and experimentation that is now possible will allow for rapid innovation and pave the way for intelligence in cloud-connected devices all around us.

When I started my career in 1995, it took a large organization to build and deploy credit card fraud detection systems. With tools like Azure ML and the power of the cloud, a single talented data scientist can accomplish the same feat. The authors of this book, who have long experience with data science, have designed it to help you get started on this wonderful journey with Azure ML.

—Joseph Sirosh
Corporate Vice President, Machine Learning, Microsoft Corporation.

Introduction

Data science and machine learning are in high demand, as customers are increasingly looking for ways to glean insights from their data. More customers now realize that business intelligence is not enough as the volume, speed, and complexity of data now defy traditional analytics tools. While business intelligence addresses descriptive and diagnostic analysis, data science unlocks new opportunities through predictive and prescriptive analysis.

This book provides an overview of data science and an in-depth view of Microsoft Azure Machine Learning, the latest predictive analytics service from the company. The book provides a structured approach to data science and practical guidance for solving real-world business problems such as buyer propensity modeling, customer churn analysis, predictive maintenance, and product recommendation. The simplicity of this new service from Microsoft will help to take data science and machine learning to a much broader audience than existing products in this space. Learn how you can quickly build and deploy sophisticated predictive models as machine learning web services with the new Azure Machine Learning service from Microsoft.

Who Should Read this Book?

This book is for budding data scientists, business analysts, BI professionals, and developers. The reader needs to have basic skills in statistics and data analysis. That said, they do not need to be data scientists or have deep data mining skills to benefit from this book.

What You Will Learn

This book will provide the following:

- A deep background in data science, and how to solve a business data science problem using a structured approach and best practices

- How to use Microsoft Azure Machine Learning service to effectively build and deploy predictive models as machine learning web services

- Practical examples that show how to solve typical predictive analytics problems such as propensity modeling, churn analysis, and product recommendation.

At the end of the book, you will have gained essential skills in basic data science, the data mining process, and a clear understanding of the new Microsoft Azure Machine Learning service. You'll also have the frameworks for solving practical business problems with machine learning.

PART 1

Introducing Data Science and Microsoft Azure Machine Learning

CHAPTER 1

■ ■ ■

Introduction to Data Science

So what is data science and why is it so topical? Is it just another fad that will fade away after the hype? We will start with a simple introduction to data science, defining what it is, why it matters, and why now. This chapter highlights the data science process with guidelines and best practices. It introduces some of the most commonly used techniques and algorithms in data science. And it explores ensemble models, a key technology on the cutting edge of data science.

What Is Data Science?

Data science is the practice of obtaining useful insights from data. Although it also applies to small data, data science is particularly important for big data, as we now collect petabytes of structured and unstructured data from many sources inside and outside an organization. As a result, we are now data rich but information poor. Data science provides powerful processes and techniques for gleaning actionable information from this sea of data. Data science draws from several disciplines including statistics, mathematics, operations research, signal processing, linguistics, database and storage, programming, machine learning, and scientific computing. Figure 1-1 illustrates the most common disciplines of data science. Although the term *data science* is new in business, it has been around since 1960 when it was first used by Peter Naur to refer to data processing methods in Computer Science. Since the late 1990s notable statisticians such as C.F. Jeff Wu and William S. Cleveland have also used the term data science, a discipline they view as the same as or an extension of statistics.

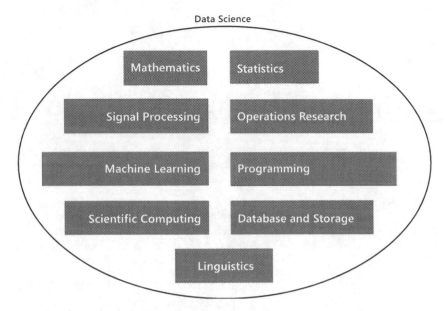

Figure 1-1. *Highlighting the main academic disciplines that constitute data science*

Practitioners of data science are data scientists, whose skills span statistics, mathematics, operations research, signal processing, linguistics, database and storage, programming, machine learning, and scientific computing. In addition, to be effective, data scientists need good communication and data visualization skills. Domain knowledge is also important to deliver meaningful results. This breadth of skills is very hard to find in one person, which is why data science is a team sport, not an individual effort. To be effective, one needs to hire a team with complementary data science skills.

Analytics Spectrum

According to Gartner, all the analytics we do can be classified into one of four categories: descriptive, diagnostic, predictive, and prescriptive analysis. Descriptive analysis typically helps to describe a situation and can help to answer questions like *What happened?, Who are my customers*?, etc. Diagnostic analysis help you understand why things happened and can answer questions like *Why did it happen?* Predictive analysis is forward-looking and can answer questions such as *What will happen in the future?* As the name suggests, prescriptive analysis is much more prescriptive and helps answer questions like *What should we do?, What is the best route to my destination?*, or *How should I allocate my investments?*

Figure 1-2 illustrates the full analytics spectrum. It also shows the degree of sophistication in this diagram.

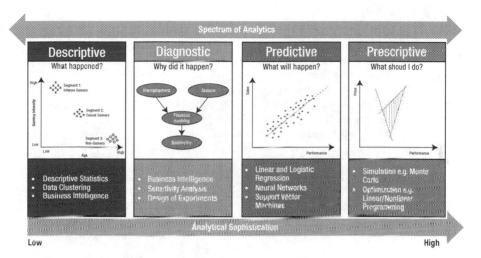

Figure 1-2. *Spectrum of all data analysis*

Descriptive Analysis

Descriptive analysis is used to explain what is happening in a given situation. This class of analysis typically involves human intervention and can be used to answer questions like *What happened?, Who are my customers?, How many types of users do we have?*, etc. Common techniques used for this include descriptive statistics with charts, histograms, box and whisker plots, or data clustering. You'll explore these techniques later in this chapter.

Diagnostic Analysis

Diagnostic analysis helps you understand why certain things happened and what are the key drivers. For example, a wireless provider would use this to answer questions such as *Why are dropped calls increasing?* or *Why are we losing more customers every month?* A customer diagnostic analysis can be done with techniques such as clustering, classification, decision trees, or content analysis. These techniques are available in statistics, data mining, and machine learning. It should be noted that business intelligence is also used for diagnostic analysis.

Predictive Analysis

Predictive analysis helps you predict what will happen in the future. It is used to predict the probability of an uncertain outcome. For example, it can be used to predict if a credit card transaction is fraudulent, or if a given customer is likely to upgrade to a premium phone plan. Statistics and machine learning offer great techniques for prediction. This includes techniques such as neural networks, decision trees, monte carlo simulation, and regression.

Prescriptive Analysis

Prescriptive analysis will suggest the best course of action to take to optimize your business outcomes. Typically, prescriptive analysis combines a predictive model with business rules (e.g. decline a transaction if the probability of fraud is above a given threshold). For example, it can suggest the best phone plan to offer a given customer, or based on optimization, can propose the best route for your delivery trucks. Prescriptive analysis is very useful in scenarios such as channel optimization, portfolio optimization, or traffic optimization to find the best route given current traffic conditions. Techniques such as decision trees, linear and non-linear programming, monte carlo simulation, or game theory from statistics and data mining can be used to do prescriptive analysis. See Figure 1-2.

The analytical sophistication increases from descriptive to prescriptive analytics. In many ways, prescriptive analytics is the nirvana of analytics and is often used by the most analytically sophisticated organizations. Imagine a smart telecommunications company that has embedded analytical models in its business workflow systems. It has the following analytical models embedded in its customer call center system:

- **A customer churn model**: This is a predictive model that predicts the probability of customer attrition. In other words, it predicts the likelihood of the customer calling the call center ultimately defecting to the competition.

- **A customer segmentation model**: This segments customers into distinct segments for marketing purposes.

- **A customer propensity model**: This model predicts the customer's propensity to respond to each of the marketing offers, such as upgrades to premium plans.

When a customer calls, the call center system identifies him or her in real time from their cell phone number. Then the call center system scores the customer using these three models. If the customer scores high on the customer churn model, it means they are very likely to defect to the competitor. In that case, the telecommunications company will immediately route the customer to a group of call center agents who are empowered to make attractive offers to prevent attrition. Otherwise, if the segmentation model scores the customer as a profitable customer, he/she is routed to a special concierge service with shorter wait lines and the best customer service. If the propensity model scores the customer high for upgrades, the call agent is alerted and will try to upsell the customer with attractive upgrades. The beauty of this solution is that all the models are baked into the telecommunication company's business workflow, driving their agents to make smart decisions that improve profitability and customer satisfaction. This is illustrated in Figure 1-3.

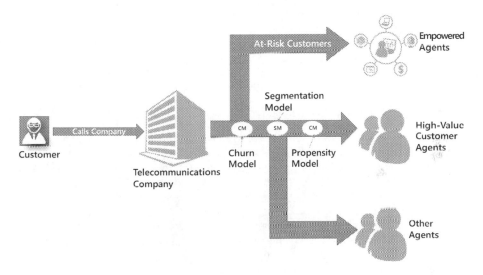

Figure 1-3. *A smart telco using prescriptive analytics*

Why Does It Matter and Why Now?

Data science offers customers a real opportunity to make smarter and timely decisions based on all the data they collect. With the right tools, data science offers customers new and actionable insights not only from their own data, but also from the growing sources of data outside their organizations, such as weather data, customer demographic data, consumer credit data from the credit bureaus, and data from social media sites such as Twitter, Instagram, etc. Here are a few reasons why data science is now critical for business success.

Data as a Competitive Asset

Data is now a critical asset that offers a competitive advantage to smart organizations that use it correctly for decision making. McKinsey and Gartner agree on this: in a recent paper McKinsey suggests that companies that use data and business analytics to make decisions are more productive and deliver a higher return on equity than those who don't. In a similar vein, Gartner posits that organizations that invest in a modern data infrastructure will outperform their peers by up to 20%. Big data offers organizations the opportunity to combine valuable data across silos to glean new insights that drive smarter decisions.

> *"Companies that use data and business analytics to guide decision making are more productive and experience higher returns on equity than competitors that don't"*
>
> —Brad Brown et al., McKinsey Global Institute, 2011

"By 2015, organizations integrating high-value, diverse, new information types and sources into a coherent information management infrastructure will outperform their industry peers financially by more than 20%."

—Regina Casonato et al., Gartner[1]

Increased Customer Demand

Business intelligence has been the key form of analytics used by most organizations in the last few decades. However, with the emergence of big data, more customers are now eager to use predictive analytics to improve marketing and business planning. Traditional BI gives a good rear view analysis of their business, but does not help with any forward-looking questions that include forecasting or prediction.

The past two years have seen a surge of demand from customers for predictive analytics as they seek more powerful analytical techniques to uncover value from the troves of data they store on their businesses. In our combined experience we have not seen as much demand for data science from customers as we did in the last two years alone!

Increased Awareness of Data Mining Technologies

Today a subset of data mining and machine learning algorithms are now more widely understood since they have been tried and tested by early adopters such as Netflix and Amazon, who use them in their recommendation engines. While most customers do not fully understand details of the machine learning algorithms used, their application in Netflix movie recommendations or recommendation engines at online stores are very salient. Similarly, many customers are now aware of the targeted ads that are now heavily used by most sophisticated online vendors. So while many customers may not know details of the algorithms used, they now increasingly understand their business value.

Access to More Data

Digital data has been exploding in the last few years and shows no signs of abating. Most industry pundits now agree that we are collecting more data than ever before. According to IDC, the digital universe will grow to 35 zetabytes (i.e. 35 trillion terabytes) globally by 2020. Others posit that the world's data is now growing by up to 10 times every 5 years, which is astounding. In a recent study, McKinsey Consulting also found that in 15 of the 17 US economic sectors, companies with over 1,000 employees store, on average, over 235 terabytes of data–which is more than the data stored by the US Library of Congress! This data explosion is driven by the rise of new data sources such as social media, cell phones, smart sensors, and dramatic gains in the computer industry.

The large volumes of data being collected also enables you to build more accurate predictive models. We know from statistics that the confidence interval (also known as the margin of error) has an inverse relationship with the sample size. So the larger your sample size, the smaller the margin of error. This in turn increases the accuracy of predictions from your model.

Faster and Cheaper Processing Power

We now have far more computing power at our disposal than ever before. Moore's Law proposed that computer chip performance would grow exponentially, doubling every 18 months. This trend has been true for most of the history of modern computing. In 2010, the International Technology Roadmap for Semiconductors updated this forecast, predicting that growth would slow down in 2013 when computer densities and counts would double every 3 years instead of 18 months. Despite this, the exponential growth in processor performance has delivered dramatic gains in technology and economic productivity. Today, a smartphone's processor is up to five times more powerful than that of a desktop computer 20 years ago. For instance, the Nokia Lumia 928 has a dual-core 1.5 GHz Qualcomm Snapdragon™ S4 that is at least five times faster than the Intel Pentium P5 CPU released in 1993, which was very popular for personal computers. In the nineties, expensive workstations like the DEC VAX mainframes or the DEC Alpha workstations were required to run advanced, compute-intensive algorithms. It is remarkable that today's smartphone is also five times faster than the powerful DEC Alpha processor from 1994 whose speed was 200 300 MHz! Today you can run the same algorithms on affordable personal workstations with multi-core processors. In addition, we can leverage Hadoop's MapReduce architecture to deploy powerful data mining algorithms on a farm of commodity servers at a much lower cost than ever before. With data science we now have the tools to discover hidden patterns in our data through smart deployment of data mining and machine learning algorithms.

We have also seen dramatic gains in capacity, and an exponential drop in the price of computer memory. This is illustrated in Figures 1-4 and 1-5, which show the exponential price drop and growth in capacity of computer memory since 1960. Since 1990 the average price per MB of memory has dropped from $59 to a meager 0.49 cents–a 99.2% price reduction! At the same time, the capacity of a memory module has increased from 8MB to a whopping 8GB! As a result, a modest laptop is now more powerful than a high-end workstation from the early nineties.

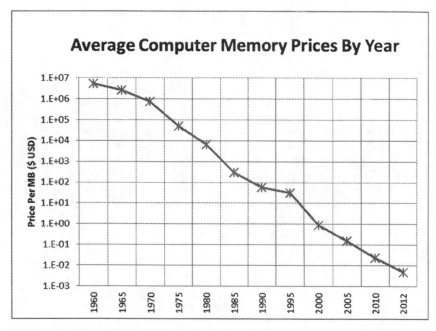

Figure 1-4. *Average computer memory price since 1960*

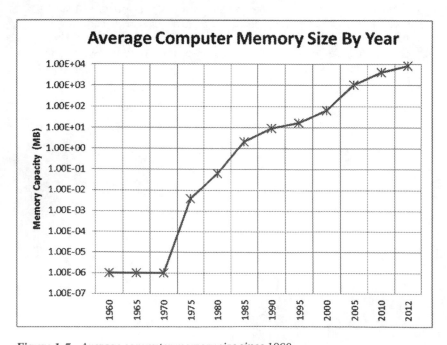

Figure 1-5 *Average computer memory size since 1960*

▓ **Note**　For more information on memory price history is available at John C. McCallum: http://www.jcmit.com/mem2012.htm.

The Data Science Process

A typical data science project follows the five-step process outlined in Figure 1-6. Let's review each of these steps in detail.

1. **Define the business problem**: This is critical as it guides the rest of the project. Before building any models, it is important to work with the project sponsor to identify the specific business problem he or she is trying to solve. Without this, one could spend weeks or months building sophisticated models that solve the wrong problem, leading to wasted effort. A good data science project gleans good insights that drive smarter business decisions. Hence the analysis should serve a business goal. It should not be a hammer in search of a nail! There are formal consulting techniques and frameworks (such as guided discovery workshops and six sigma methodology) used by practitioners to help business stakeholders prioritize and scope their business goals.

2. **Acquire and prepare data**: This step entails two activities. The first is the acquisition of raw data from several source systems including databases, CRM systems, web log files, etc. This may involve ETL (extract, transform, and load) processes, database administrators, and BI personnel. However, the data scientist is intimately involved to ensure the right data is extracted in the right format. Working with the raw data also provides vital context that is required downstream. Second, once the right data is pulled, it is analyzed and prepared for modelling. This involves addressing missing data, outliers in the data, and data transformations. Typically, if a variable has over 40% of missing values, it can be rejected, unless the fact that it is missing (or not) conveys critical information. For example, there might be a strong bias in the demographics of who fills in the optional field of "age" in a survey. For the rest, we need to decide how to deal with missing values; should we impute with the average value, median or something else? There are several statistical techniques for detecting outliers. With a box and whisker plot, an outlier is a sample (value) greater or smaller than 1.5 times the interquartile range (IQR). The interquartile range is the 75th percentile-25th percentile. We need to decide whether to drop an outlier or not. If it makes sense to keep it, we need to find a useful transformation for the variable. For instance, log transformation is generally useful for transforming incomes.

11

Correlation analysis, principal component analysis, or factor analysis are useful techniques that show the relationships between the variables. Finally, feature selection is done at this stage to identify the right variables to use in the model in the next step.

This step can be laborious and time-consuming. In fact, in a typical data science project, we spend up to 75 to 80% of time in data acquisition and preparation. That said, it is the vital step that coverts raw data into high quality gems for modelling. The old adage is still true: *garbage in, garbage out*. Investing wisely in data preparation improves the success of your project.

3. **Develop the model**: This is the most fun part of the project where we develop the predictive models. In this step, we determine the right algorithm to use for modeling given the business problem and data. For instance, if it is a binary classification problem we can use logistic regression, decision trees, boosted decision trees, or neural networks. If the final model has to be explainable, this rules out algorithms like boosted decision trees. Model building is an iterative process: we experiment with different models to find the most predictive one. We also validate it with the customer a few times to ensure it meets their needs before exiting this stage.

4. **Deploy the model**: Once built, the final model has to be deployed in production where it will be used to score transactions or by customers to drive real business decisions. Models are deployed in many different ways depending on the customer's environment. In most cases, deploying a model involves reimplementing the data transformations and predictive algorithm developed by the data scientist in order to integrate with an existing decision management platform. Suffice to say is a cumbersome process today. Azure Machine Learning dramatically simplifies model deployment by enabling data scientists to deploy their finished models as web services that can be invoked from any application on any platform, including mobile devices.

5. **Monitor model's performance**: Data science does not end with deployment. It is worth noting that every statistical or machine learning model is only an approximation of the real world, and hence is imperfect from the very beginning. When a validated model is tested and deployed in production, it has to be monitored to ensure it is performing as planned. This is critical because any data-driven model has a fixed shelf life. The accuracy of the model degrades with time because fundamentally the data in production will vary over time for a number of reasons, such as the business may launch new products to target a different demographic. For instance, the wireless carrier we discussed earlier may choose to launch a new phone plan for teenage kids.

If they continue to use the same churn and propensity models, they may see a degradation in their models' performance after the launch of this new product. This is because the original dataset used to build the churn and propensity models did not contain significant numbers of teenage customers. With close monitoring of the model in production we can detect when its performance starts to degrade. When its accuracy degrades significantly, it is time to rebuild the model by either re-training it with the latest dataset including production data, or completely rebuilding it with additional datasets. In that case, we return to Step 1 where we revisit the business goals and start all over.

How often should we rebuild a model? The frequency varies by business domain. In a stable business environment where the data does not vary too quickly, models can be rebuilt once every year or two. A good example is retail banking products such as mortgages and car loans. However, in a very dynamic environment where the ambient data changes rapidly, models can be rebuilt daily or weekly. A good case in point is the wireless phone industry, which is fiercely competitive. Churn models need to be retrained every few days since customers are being lured by ever more attractive offers from the competition.

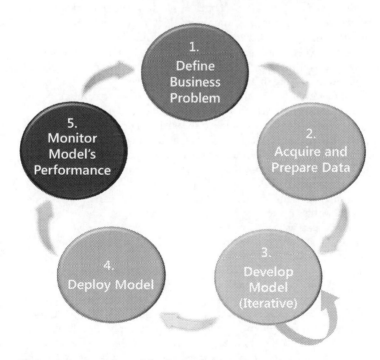

Figure 1-6. Overview of the data science process

Common Data Science Techniques

Data science offers a large body of algorithms from its constituent disciplines, namely statistics, mathematics, operations research, signal processing, linguistics, database and storage, programming, machine learning, and scientific computing. We organize these algorithms into the following groups for simplicity:

- Classification

- Clustering

- Regression

- Simulation

- Content analysis

- Recommenders

Chapter 4 provides more details on some of these algorithms.

Classification Algorithms

Classification algorithms are commonly used to classify people or things into one of many groups. They are also widely used for predictions. For example, to prevent fraud, a card issuer will classify a credit card transactions as either fraudulent or not. The card issuer typically has a large volume of historical credit card transactions and knows the status of each of these transactions. Many of these cases are reported by the legitimate cardholder who does not want to pay for unauthorized charges. So the issuer knows whether each transaction was fraudulent or not. Using this historical data the issuer can now build a model that predicts whether a new credit card transaction is likely to be fraudulent or not. This is a binary classification problem in which all cases fall into one of two classes.

Another classification problem is the customers' propensity to upgrade to a premium phone plan. In this case, the wireless carrier needs to know if a customer will upgrade to a premium plan or not. Using sales and usage data, the carrier can determine which customers upgraded in the past. Hence they can classify all customers into one of two groups: whether they upgraded or not. Since the carrier also has information on demographic and behavioral data on new and existing customers, they can build a model to predict a new customer's probability to upgrade; in other words, the model will group each customer into one of two classes.

Statistics and data mining offer many great tools for classification: this includes logistic regression, which is widely used by statisticians for building credit scorecards, or propensity-to-buy models, or neural networks algorithms such as backpropagation, radial basis functions, or ridge polynomial networks. Others include decision trees or ensemble models such as boosted decision trees or random forests. For more complex classification problems with more than two classes you can use multimodal techniques that predict multiple classes. Classification problems generally use supervised learning algorithms that use label data for training. Azure Machine Learning offers several algorithms for classification including logistic regression, decision trees, boosted decision trees, multimodal neural networks, etc. See Chapter 4 for more details.

Clustering Algorithms

Clustering uses unsepuervised learning to group data into distinct classes. A major difference between clustering and classification problems is that the outcome of clustering is unknown beforehand. Before clustering we do not know the cluster to which each data point belongs. In contrast, with classification problems we have historical data that shows to which class each a data point belongs. For example, the lender knows from historical data whether a customer defaulted on their car loans or not.

A good application of clustering is customer segmentation where we group customers into distinct segments for marketing purposes. In a good segmentation model, the data within each segment is very similar. However, data across different segments is very different. For example, a marketer in the gaming segment needs to understand his or her customers better in order to create the right offers for them. Let's assume that he or she only has two variables on the customers, namely age and gaming intensity. Using clustering, the marketer finds that there are three distinct segments of gaming customers, as shown in Figure 1-7. Segment 1 is the intense gamers who play computer games passionately every day and are typically young. Segment 2 is the casual gamers who only play occasionally and are typically in their thirties or forties. The non-gamers rarely ever play computer games and are typically older; they make up Segment 3.

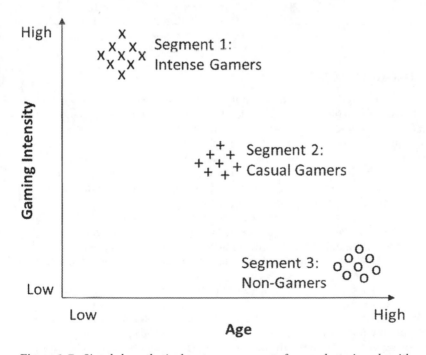

Figure 1-7. *Simple hypothetical customer segments from a clustering algorithm*

15

Statistics offers several tools for clustering, but the most widely used is the k-means algorithm that uses a distance metric to cluster similar data together. With this algorithm you decide apriori how many clusters you want; this is the constant K. If you set K = 3, the algorithm produces three clusters. Refer to Haralambos Marmanis and Dmitry Babenko's book for more details on the k-means algorithm. Machine learning also offers more sophisticated algorithms such as self-organizing maps (also known as Kohonen networks) developed by Teuvo Kohonen, or adaptive resonance theory (ART) networks developed by Stephen Grossberg and Gail Carpenter. Clustering algorithms typically use unsupervised learning since the outcome is not known during training.

■ **Note**   You can read more about clustering algorithms in the following books and paper:

"Algorithms of the Intelligent Web", Haralambos Marmanis and Dmitry Babenko. Manning Publications Co., Stamford CT. January 2011.

"Self-Organizing Maps. Third, extended edition". Springer. Kohonen, T. 2001.

"Art2-A: an adaptive resonance algorithm for rapid category learning and recognition", Carpenter, G., Grossberg, S., and Rosen, D. Neural Networks, 4:493-504. 1991a.

Regression Algorithms

Regression techniques are used to predict response variables with numerical outcomes. For example, a wireless carrier can use regression techniques to predict call volumes at their customer service centers. With this information they can allocate the right number of call center staff to meet demand. The input variables for regression models may be numeric or categorical. However, what is common with these algorithms is that the output (or response variable) is typically numeric. Some of the most commonly used regression techniques include linear regression, decision trees, neural networks, and boosted decision tree regression.

Linear regression is one of the oldest prediction techniques in statistics and its goal is to predict a given outcome from a set of observed variables. A simple linear regression model is a linear function. If there is only one input variable, the linear regression model is the best line that fits the data. For two or more input variables, the regression model is the best hyperplane that fits the underlying data.

Artificial neural networks are a set of algorithms that mimic the functioning of the brain. They learn by example and can be trained to make predictions from a dataset even when the function that maps the response to independent variables is unknown. There are many different neural network algorithms, including backpropagation networks, and radial basis function (RBF). However, the most common is backpropagation, also known as multilayered perceptron. Neural networks are used for regression or classification.

Decision tree algorithms are hierarchical techniques that work by splitting the dataset iteratively based on certain statistical criteria. The goal of decision trees is to maximize the variance across different nodes in the tree, and minimize the variance within each node. Some of the most commonly used decision tree algorithms include Iterative Dichotomizer 3 (ID3), C4.5 and C5.0 (successors of ID3), Automatic Interaction Detection (AID), Chi Squared Automatic Interaction Detection (CHAID), and Classification and Regression Tree (CART). While very useful, the ID3, C4.5, C5.0, and CHAID algorithms are classification algorithms and are not useful for regression. The CART algorithm, on the other hand, can be used for either classification or regression.

Simulation

Simulation is widely used across many industries to model and optimize processes in the real world. Engineers have long used mathematical techniques like finite elements or finite volumes to simulate the aerodynamics of aircraft wings or cars. Simulation saves engineering firms millions of dollars in R&D costs since they no longer have to do all their testing with real physical models. In addition, simulation offers the opportunity to test many more scenarios by simply adjusting variables in their computer models.

In business, simulation is used to model processes like optimizing wait times in call centers or optimizing routes for trucking companies or airlines. Through simulation, business analysts can model a vast set of hypotheses to optimize for profit or other business goals.

Statistics offers many powerful techniques for simulation and optimization: Markov chain analysis can be used to simulate state changes in a dynamic system. For instance, it can be used to model how customers will flow through a call center: how long will a customer wait before dropping off, or what are their chances of staying on after engaging the interactive voice response (IVR) system? Linear programming is used to optimize trucking or airline routes, while Monte Carlo simulation is used to find the best conditions to optimize for given business outcome such as profit.

Content Analysis

Content analysis is used to mine content such as text files, images, and videos for insights. Text mining uses statistical and linguistic analysis to understand the meaning of text. Simple keyword searching is too primitive for most practical applications. For example, to understand the sentiment of Twitter feed data with a simple keyword search is a manual and laborious process because you have to store keywords for positive, neutral, and negative sentiments. Then as you scan the Twitter data, you score each Twitter feed based on the specific keywords detected. This approach, though useful in narrow cases, is cumbersome and fairly primitive. The process can be automated with text mining and natural language processing (NLP) that mines the text and tries to infer the meaning of words based on context instead of simple keyword search.

Machine learning also offers several tools for analyzing images and videos through pattern recognition. Through pattern recognition, we can identify known targets with face recognition algorithms. Neural network algorithms such as multilayer perceptron and ART networks can be used to detect and track known targets in video streams, or to aid analysis of x-ray images.

Recommendation Engines

Recommendation engines have been used extensively by online retailers like Amazon to recommend products based on users' preferences. There are three broad approaches to recommendation engines. Collaborative filtering (CF) makes recommendations based on similarities between users or items. With item-based collaborative filtering, we analyze item data to find which items are similar. With collaborative filtering, that data is specifically the interactions of users with the movies, for example ratings or viewing, as opposed to characteristics of the movies such as genre, director, actors. So whenever a customer buys a movie from this set we recommend others based on similarity.

The second class of recommendation engines makes recommendations by analyzing the content selected by each user. In this case, text mining or natural language processing techniques are used to analyze content such as document files. Similar content types are grouped together, and this forms the basis of recommendations to new users. More information on collaborative filtering and content-based approaches are available in Haralambos Marmanis and Dmitry Babenko's book.

The third approach to recommendation engines uses sophisticated machine learning algorithms to determine product affinity. This approach is also known as market basket analysis. Algorithms such as Naïve Bayes or the Microsoft Association Rules are used to mine sales data to determine which products sell together.

Cutting Edge of Data Science

Let's conclude this chapter with a quick overview of ensemble models that are at the cutting edge of data science.

The Rise of Ensemble Models

Ensemble models are a set of classifiers from machine learning that use a panel of algorithms instead of a single one to solve classification problems. They mimic our human tendency to improve the accuracy of decisions by consulting knowledgeable friends or experts. When faced with important decisions such as a medical diagnosis, we tend to seek a second opinion from other doctors to improve our confidence. In the same way, ensemble models use a set of algorithms as a panel of experts to improve the accuracy and reduce the variance of classification problems.

The machine learning community has worked on ensemble models for decades. In fact, seminal papers were published as early as 1979 by Dasarathy and Sheela. However, since the mid-1990s, this area has seen rapid progress with several important contributions resulting in very successful real world applications.

Real World Applications of Ensemble Models

In the last few years ensemble models have been found in great real-world applications including face recognition in cameras, bioinformatics, Netflix movie recommendations, and Microsoft's Xbox Kinect. Let's examine two of these applications.

First, ensemble models were very instrumental to the success of the Netflix Prize competition. In 2006, Netflix ran an open contest with a $1 million prize for the best collaborative filtering algorithm that improved their existing solution by 10%. In September 2009 the $1 million prize was awarded to BellKor's Pragmatic Chaos, a team of scientists from AT&T Labs joining forces with two lesser known teams. At the start of the contest, most teams used single classifier algorithms: although they outperformed the Netflix model by 6–8%, performance quickly plateaued until teams started applying ensemble models. Leading contestants soon realized that they could improve their models by combining their algorithms with those of the apparently weaker teams. In the end, most of the top teams, including the winners, used ensemble models to significantly outperform Netflix's recommendation engine. For example, the second-place team used more than 900 individual models in their ensemble.

Microsoft's Xbox Kinect sensor also uses ensemble modeling. Random Forests, a form of ensemble model, is used effectively to track skeletal movements when users play games with the Xbox Kinect sensor.

Despite success in real-world applications, a key limitation of ensemble models is that they are black boxes in that their decisions are hard to explain. As a result, they are not suitable for applications where decisions have to be explained. Credit scorecards are a good example because lenders need to explain the credit score they assign to each consumer. In some markets, such explanations are a legal requirement and hence ensemble models would be unsuitable despite their predictive power.

Building an Ensemble Model

There are three key steps to building an ensemble model: a) selecting data, b) training classifiers, and c) combining classifiers.

The first step to build an ensemble model is data selection for the classifier models. When sampling the data, a key goal is to maximize diversity of the models, since this improves the accuracy of the solution. In general, the more diverse your models, the better the performance of your final classifier, and the smaller the variance of its predictions.

Step 2 of the process entails training several individual classifiers. But how do you assign the classifiers? Of the many available strategies, the two most popular are bagging and boosting. The bagging algorithm uses different subsets of the data to train each model. The Random Forest algorithm uses this bagging approach. In contrast, the boosting algorithm improves performance by making misclassified examples in the training set more important during training. So during training, each additional model focuses on the misclassified data. The boosted decision tree algorithm uses the boosting strategy.

Finally, once you train all the classifiers, the final step is to combine their results to make a final prediction. There are several approaches to combining the outcomes, ranging from a simple majority to a weighted majority voting.

Ensemble models are a really exciting part of machine learning with the potential for breakthroughs in classification problems.

Summary

This chapter introduced data science, defining what it is, why it matters, and why now. We outlined the key academic disciplines of data science, including statistics, mathematics, operations research, signal processing, linguistics, database and storage, programming, and machine learning. We covered the key reasons behind the heightened interest in data science: increasing data volumes, data as a competitive asset, growing awareness of data mining, and hardware economics.

A simple five-step data science process was introduced with guidelines on how to apply it correctly. We also introduced some of the most commonly used techniques and algorithms in data science. Finally, we introduced ensemble models, which is one of the key technologies on the cutting edge of data science.

Bibliography

1. Alexander Linden, 2014. Key trends and emerging technologies in advanced analytics. Gartner BI Summit 2014, Las Vegas, USA.

2. "Are you ready for the era of Big Data?", McKinsey Global Institute - Brad Brown, Michael Chui, and James Manyika, October 2011.

3. "Information Management in the 21st Century", Gartner - Regina Casonato, Anne Lapkin, Mark A. Beyer, Yvonne Genovese, Ted Friedman, September 2011.

4. John C. McCallum: http://www.jcmit.com/mem2012.htm.

5. "Algorithms of the Intelligent Web", Haralambos Marmanis and Dmitry Babenko. Manning Publications Co., Stamford CT. January 2011.

6. "Self-Organizing Maps. Third, extended edition". Springer. Kohonen, T. 2001.

7. "Art2-A: an adaptive resonance algorithm for rapid category learning and recognition", Carpenter, G., Grossberg, S., and Rosen, D. Neural Networks, 4:493–504. 1991a.

8. "Data Mining with Microsoft SQL Server 2008", Jamie MacLennan, ZhaoHui Tang and Bogdan Crivat. Wiley Publishing Inc, Indianapolis, Indiana, 2009.

■ ■ ■

## CHAPTER 2

Introducing Microsoft Azure Machine Learning

Azure Machine Learning, where data science, predictive analytics, cloud computing, and your data meet!

Azure Machine Learning empowers data scientists and developers to transform data into insights using predictive analytics. By making it easier for developers to use the predictive models in end-to-end solutions, Azure Machine Learning enables actionable insights to be gleaned and operationalized easily.

Using Machine Learning Studio, data scientists and developers can quickly build, test, and develop the predictive models using state-of-the art machine learning algorithms.

Hello, Machine Learning Studio!

Azure Machine Learning Studio provides an interactive visual workspace that enables you to easily build, test, and deploy predictive analytic models.

In Machine Learning Studio, you construct a predictive model by dragging and dropping datasets and analysis modules onto the design surface. You can iteratively build predictive analytic models using experiments in Azure Machine Learning Studio. Each experiment is a complete workflow with all the components required to build, test, and evaluate a predictive model. In an experiment, machine learning modules are connected together with lines that show the flow of data and parameters through the workflow. Once you design an experiment, you can use Machine Learning Studio to execute it.

Machine Learning Studio allows you to iterate rapidly by building and testing several models in minutes. When building an experiment, it is common to iterate on the design of the predictive model, edit the parameters or modules, and run the experiment several times.

Often, you will save multiple copies of the experiment (using different parameters). When you first open Machine Learning Studio, you will notice it is organized as follows:

- **Experiments**: Experiments that have been created, run, and saved as drafts. These include a set of sample experiments that ship with the service to help jumpstart your projects.

- **Web Services**: A list of experiments that you have published as web services. This list will be empty until you publish your first experiment.

- **Settings**: A collection of settings that you can use to configure your account and resources. You can use this option to invite other users to share your workspace in Azure Machine Learning.

To develop a predictive model, you will need to be able to work with data from different data sources. In addition, the data needs to be transformed and analyzed before it can be used as input for training the predictive model. Various data manipulation and statistical functions are used for preprocessing the data and identifying the parts of the data that are useful. As you develop a model, you go through an iterative process where you use various techniques to understand the data, the key features in the data, and the parameters that are used to tune the machine learning algorithms. You continuously iterate on this until you get to point where you have a trained and effective model that can be used.

Components of an Experiment

An experiment is made of the key components necessary to build, test, and evaluate a predictive model. In Azure Machine Learning, an experiment contains two main components: datasets and modules.

A dataset contains data that has been uploaded to Machine Learning Studio. The dataset is used when creating a predictive model. Machine Learning Studio also provides several sample datasets to help you jumpstart the creation of your first few experiments. As you explore Machine Learning Studio, you can upload additional datasets.

A module is an algorithm that you will use when building your predictive model. Machine Learning Studio provides a large set of modules to support the end-to-end data science workflow, from reading data from different data sources; preprocessing the data; to building, training, scoring, and validating a predictive model. These modules include the following:

- **Convert to ARFF**: Converts a .NET serialized dataset to ARFF format.

- **Convert to CSV**: Converts a .NET serialized dataset to CSV format.

- **Reader**: This module is used to read data from several sources including the Web, Azure SQL Database, Azure Blob storage, or Hive tables.

- **Writer**: This module is used to write data to Azure SQL Database, Azure Blob storage, or Hadoop Distributed File system (HDFS).

- **Moving Average Filter**: This creates a moving average of a given dataset.

- **Join**: This module joins two datasets based on keys specified by the user. It does inner joins, left outer joins, full outer joins, and left semi-joins of the two datasets.

- **Split**: This module splits a dataset into two parts. It is typically used to split a dataset into separate training and test datasets.

- **Filter-Based Feature Selection**: This module is used to find the most important variables for modeling. It uses seven different techniques (e.g. Spearman Correlation, Pearson Correlation, Mutual Information, Chi Squared, etc.) to rank the most important variables from raw data.

- **Elementary Statistics**: Calculates elementary statistics such as the mean, standard deviation, etc., of a given dataset.

- **Linear Regression**: Can be used to create a predictive model with a linear regression algorithm.

- **Train Model**: This module trains a selected classification or regression algorithm with a given training dataset.

- **Sweep Parameters**: For a given learning algorithm, along with training and validation datasets, this module finds parameters that result in the best trained model.

- **Evaluate Model**: This module is used to evaluate the performance of a trained classification or regression model.

- **Cross Validate Model**: This module is used to perform cross-validation to avoid over fitting. By default this module uses 10-fold cross-validation.

- **Score Model**: Scores a trained classification or regression model.

All available modules are organized under the menus shown in Figure 2-1. Each module provides a set of parameters that you can use to fine-tune the behavior of the algorithm used by the module. When a module is selected, you will see the parameters for the module displayed on the right pane of the canvas.

Five Easy Steps to Creating an Experiment

In this section, you will learn how to use Azure Machine Learning Studio to develop a simple predictive analytics model. To design an experiment, you assemble a set of components that are used to create, train, test, and evaluate the model. In addition, you might leverage additional modules to preprocess the data, perform feature selection and/or reduction, split the data into training and test sets, and evaluate or cross-validate the model. The following five basic steps can be used as a guide for creating an experiment.

Create a Model

> Step 1: Get data
>
> Step 2: Preprocess data
>
> Step 3: Define features

Train the Model

> Step 4: Choose and apply a learning algorithm

Test the Model

> Step 5: Predict over new data

Step 1: Get Data

Azure Machine Learning Studio provides a number of sample datasets. In addition, you can also import data from many different sources. In this example, you will use the included sample dataset called **Automobile price data (Raw)**, which represents automobile price data.

1. To start a new experiment, click +**NEW** at the bottom of the Machine Learning Studio window and select **EXPERIMENT**.

2. Rename the experiment to "Chapter 02 – Hello ML".

3. To the left of the Machine Learning Studio, you will see a list of experiment items (see Figure 2-1). Click **Saved Datasets**, and type "automobile" in the search box. Find **Automobile price data (Raw)**.

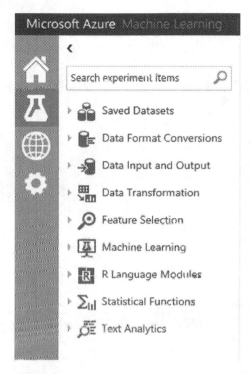

Figure 2-1. *Palette search*

4. Drag the dataset into the experiment. You can also double-click the dataset to include it in the experiment (see Figure 2-2).

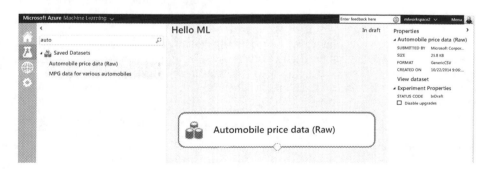

Figure 2-2. *Using a dataset*

By clicking the output port of the dataset, you can select **Visualize**, which will allow you to explore the data and understand the key statistics of each of the columns (see Figure 2-3).

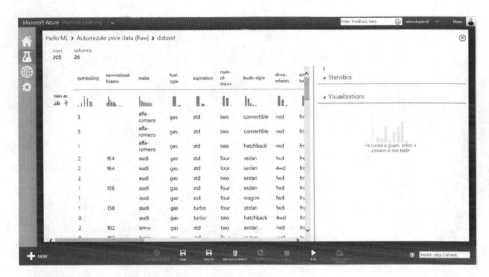

Figure 2-3. *Dataset visualization*

Close the visualization window by clicking the **x** in the upper-right corner.

Step 2: Preprocess Data

Before you start designing the experiment, it is important to preprocess the dataset. In most cases, the raw data needs to be preprocessed before it can be used as input to train a predictive analytic model.

From the earlier exploration, you may have noticed that there are missing values in the data. As a precursor to analyzing the data, these missing values need to be cleaned. For this experiment, you will substitute the missing values with a designated value. In addition, the `normalized-losses` column will be removed as this column contains too many missing values.

■ **Tip**   Cleaning the missing values from input data is a prerequisite for using most of the modules.

---

1. To remove the normalized-losses column, drag the **Project Columns** module, and connect it to the output port of the **Automobile price data (Raw)** dataset. This module allows you to select which columns of data you want to include or exclude in the model.

2. Select the **Project Columns** module and click **Launch column selector** in the properties pane (i.e. the right pane).

   a. Make sure **All columns** is selected in the filter dropdown called **Begin With**. This directs Project Columns to pass all columns through (except for the ones you are about to exclude).

   b. In the next row, select **Exclude** and **column names**, and then click inside the text box. A list of columns is displayed; select "normalized-losses" and it will be added to the text box. This is shown in Figure 2-4.

   c. Click the check mark OK button to close the column selector.

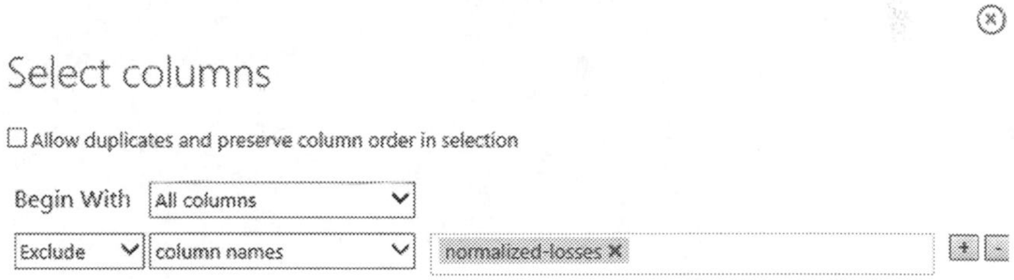

Select columns

☐ Allow duplicates and preserve column order in selection

Begin With | All columns ▾ |

| Exclude ▾ | column names ▾ | normalized-losses ✕ | ⊞ ⊟ |

Figure 2-4. *Select columns*

All columns will pass through, except for the column normalized-losses. You can see this in the properties pane for **Project Columns**. This is illustrated in Figure 2-5.

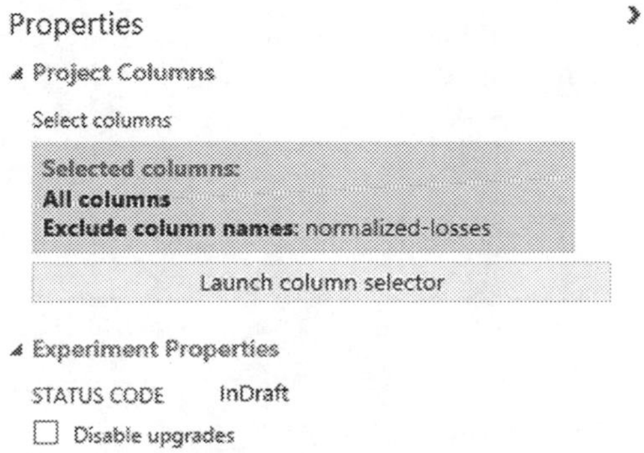

Properties   ❯

▲ Project Columns

Select columns

> **Selected columns:**
> **All columns**
> **Exclude column names:** normalized-losses

Launch column selector

▲ Experiment Properties

STATUS CODE   InDraft

☐ Disable upgrades

Figure 2-5. *Project Columns properties*

▦ **Tip**   As you design the experiment, you can add a comment to the module by double-clicking the module and entering text. This enables others to understand the purpose of each module in the experiment and can help you document your experiment design.

---

3.   Drag the **Missing Values Scrubber** module to the experiment canvas and connect it to the **Project Columns** module. You will use the default properties, which replaces the missing value with a 0. See Figure 2-6 for details.

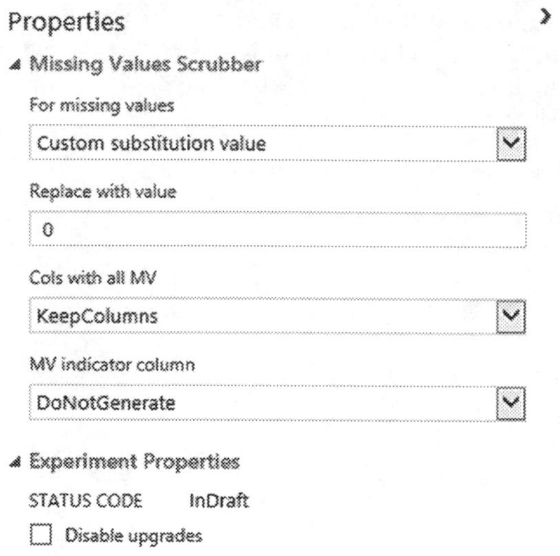

Properties   ❯

◢ Missing Values Scrubber

For missing values

| Custom substitution value | ✓ |

Replace with value

| 0 |

Cols with all MV

| KeepColumns | ✓ |

MV indicator column

| DoNotGenerate | ✓ |

◢ Experiment Properties

STATUS CODE   InDraft

☐ Disable upgrades

Figure 2-6. *Missing Values Scrubber properties*

4.   Now click **RUN**.

5.   When the experiment completes successfully, each of the modules will have a green check mark indicating its successful completion (see Figure 2-7).

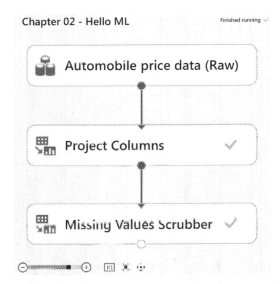

Figure 2-7. First experiment run

At this point, you have preprocessed the dataset by cleaning and transforming the data. To view the cleaned dataset, double-click the output port of the **Missing Values Scrubber** module and select **Visualize**. Notice that the normalized-losses column is no longer included, and there are no missing values.

Step 3: Define Features

In machine learning, features are individual measurable properties created from the raw data to help the algorithms to learn the task at hand. Understanding the role played by each feature is super important. For example, some features are better at predicting the target than others. In addition, some features can have a strong correlation with other features (e.g. city-mpg vs. highway-mpg). Adding highly correlated features as inputs might not be useful, since they contain similar information.

For this exercise, you will build a predictive model that uses a subset of the features of the **Automobile price data (Raw)** dataset to predict the price for new automobiles. Each row represents an automobile. Each column is a feature of that automobile. It is important to identify a good set of features that can be used to create the predictive model. Often, this requires experimentation and knowledge about the problem domain. For illustration purpose, you will use the **Project Columns** module to select the following features: make, body-style, wheel-base, engine-size, horsepower, peak-rpm, highway-mpg, and price.

1. Drag the **Project Columns** module to the experiment canvas. Connect it to the **Missing Values Scrubber** module.

2. Click **Launch column selector** in the properties pane.

3. In the column selector, select **No columns** for **Begin With**, then select **Include** and **column names** in the filter row. Enter the following column names: make, body-style, wheel-base, engine-size, horsepower, peak-rpm, highway-mpg, and price. This directs the module to pass through only these columns.

4. Click **OK**.

▦ **Tip**   As you build the experiment, you will run it. By running the experiment, you enable the column definitions of the data to be used in the **Missing Values Scrubber** module.

When you connect **Project Columns** to **Missing Values Scrubber**, the **Project Columns** module becomes aware of the column definitions in your data. When you click the column names box, a list of columns is displayed and you can then select the columns, one at a time, that you wish to add to the list.

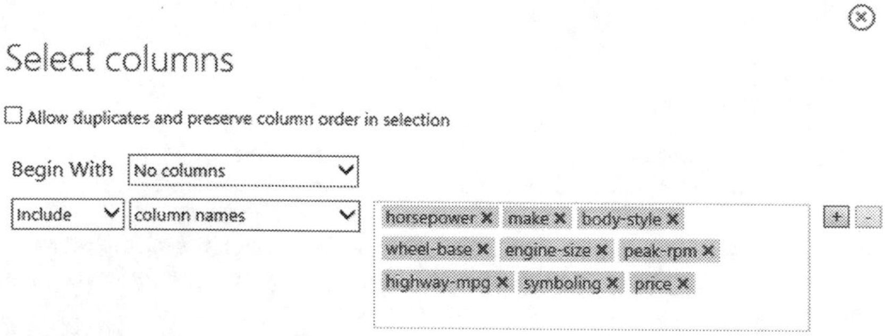

Figure 2-8. Select columns

Figure 2-8 shows the list of selected columns in the **Project Columns** module. When you train the predictive model, you need to provide the target variable. This is the feature that will be predicted by the model. For this exercise, you are predicting the price of an automobile, based on several key features of an automobile (e.g. horsepower, make, etc.)

Step 4: Choose and Apply Machine Learning Algorithms

When constructing a predictive model, you first need to train the model, and then validate that the model is effective. In this experiment, you will build a regression model.

■ **Tip** Classification and regression are two common types of predictive models. In classification, the goal is to predict if a given data row belongs to one of several classes (e.g. will a customer churn or not? Is this credit transaction fraudulent?). With regression, the goal is to predict a continuous outcome (e.g. the price of an automobile or tomorrow's temperature).

In this experiment, you will train a regression model and use it to predict the price of an automobile. Specifically, you will train a simple *linear regression* model. After the model has been trained, you will use some of the modules available in Machine Learning Studio to validate the model.

1. **Split the data into training and testing sets**: Select and drag the **Split** module to the experiment canvas and connect it to the output of the last **Project Columns** module. Set **Fraction of rows in the first output dataset** to 0.8. This way, you will use 80% of the data to train the model and hold back 20% for testing.

■ **Tip** By changing the Random seed parameter, you can produce different random samples for training and testing. This parameter controls the seeding of the pseudo-random number generator in the *Split* module.

---

2. Run the experiment. This allows the **Project Columns** and **Split** modules to pass along column definitions to the modules you will be adding next.

3. To select the learning algorithm, expand the **Machine Learning** category in the module palette to the left of the canvas and then expand **Initialize Model**. This displays several categories of modules that can be used to initialize a learning algorithm.

4. For this example experiment, select the **Linear Regression** module under the **Regression** category and drag it to the experiment canvas.

5. Find and drag the **Train Model** module to the experiment. Click **Launch column selector** and select the price column. This is the feature that your model is going to predict. Figure 2-9 shows this target selection.

Select a single column

Figure 2-9. *Select the price column*

6. Connect the output of the **Linear Regression** module to the left input port of the **Train Model** module.

7. Also, connect the training data output (i.e. the left port) of the **Split** module to the right input port of the **Train Model** module.

8. Run the experiment.

The result is a trained regression model that can be used to score new samples to make predictions. Figure 2-10 shows the experiment up to Step 7.

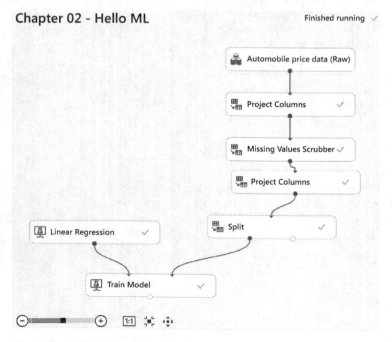

Figure 2-10. *Applying the learning algorithm*

Step 5: Predict Over New Data

Now that you've trained the model, you can use it to score the other 20% of your data and see how well your model predicts on unseen data.

1. Find and drag the **Score Model** module to the experiment canvas and connect the left input port to the output of the **Train Model** module, and the right input port to the test data output (right port) of the **Split** module. See Figure 2-11 for details.

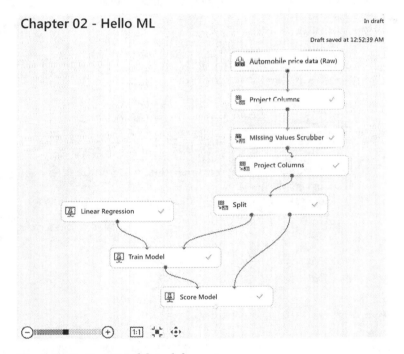

Figure 2-11. *Score Model module*

2. Run the experiment and view the output from the **Score Model** module (by double-clicking the output port and selecting **Visualize**). The output will show the predicted values for price along with the known values from the test data.

3. Finally, to test the quality of the results, select and drag the **Evaluate Model** module to the experiment canvas, and connect the left input port to the output of the **Score Model** module (there are two input ports because the **Evaluate Model** module can be used to compare two different models).

4. Run the experiment and view the output from the **Evaluate Model** module (double-click the output port and select **Visualize**). The following statistics are shown for your model:

   a. **Mean Absolute Error** (MAE): The average of absolute errors (an *error* is the difference between the predicted value and the actual value).

   b. **Root Mean Squared Error** (RMSE): The square root of the average of squared errors.

   c. **Relative Absolute Error**: The average of absolute errors relative to the absolute difference between actual values and the average of all actual values.

   d. **Relative Squared Error**: The average of squared errors relative to the squared difference between the actual values and the average of all actual values.

   e. **Coefficient of Determination**: Also known as the R squared value, this is a statistical metric indicating how well a model fits the data.

For each of the error statistics, smaller is better; a smaller value indicates that the predictions more closely match the actual values. For **Coefficient of Determination**, the closer its value is to one (1.0), the better the predictions (see Figure 2-12). If it is 1.0, this means the model explains 100% of the variability in the data, which is pretty unrealistic!

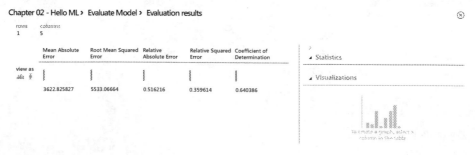

Figure 2-12. *Evaluation results*

The final experiment should look like the screenshot in Figure 2-13.

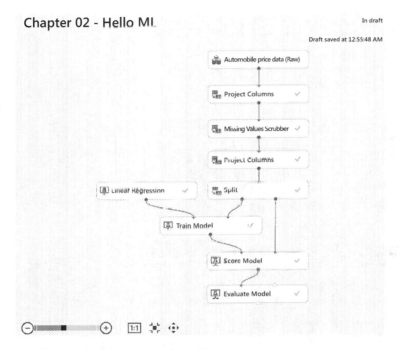

Figure 2-13. *Regression Model experiment*

Congratulations! You have created your first machine learning experiment in Machine Learning Studio. In Chapters 5-8, you will see how to apply these five steps to create predictive analytics solutions that address business challenges from different domains such as buyer propensity, churn analysis, customer segmentation, and predictive maintenance. In addition, Chapter 3 shows how to use R scripts as part of your experiments in Azure Machine Learning.

Deploying Your Model in Production

Today it takes too long to deploy machine learning models in production. The process is typically inefficient and often involves rewriting the model to run on the target production platform, which is costly and requires considerable time and effort. Azure Machine Learning simplifies the deployment of machine learning models through an integrated process in the cloud. You can deploy your new predictive model in a matter of minutes instead of days or weeks. Once deployed, your model runs as a web service that can be called from different platforms including servers, laptops, tablets, or even smartphones. To deploy your model in production follow these two steps.

1. Deploy your model to staging in Azure Machine Learning Studio.

2. In Azure Management portal, move your model from the staging environment into production.

Deploying Your Model into Staging

To deploy your model into staging, follow these steps in Azure Machine Learning Studio.

1. Save your trained mode using the **Save As** button at the bottom of Azure Machine Learning Studio. Rename it to a new name of your choice.

    a. **Run** the experiment.

    b. Right-click the output of the training module (e.g. **Train Model**) and select the option **Save As Trained Model**.

    c. Delete any modules that were used for training (e.g. **Split, Train Model, Evaluate Model**).

    d. Connect the newly saved model directly to the **Score Model** module.

    e. Rerun your experiment.

2. Before the deletion in Step 1c your experiment should appear as shown Figure 2-14.

Hello ML_Deploy

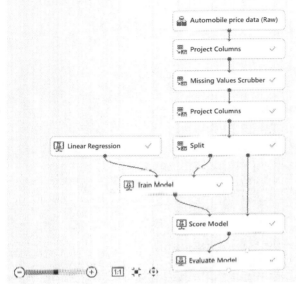

Figure 2-14. Predictive model before the training modules were deleted

After deleting the training modules (i.e. **Split, Linear Regression, Train Model,** and **Evaluate Model**) and then replacing those with the saved training model, the experiment should now appear as shown in Figure 2-15.

■ **Tip** You may be wondering why you left the **Automobile price data (Raw)** dataset connected to the model. The service is going to use the user's data, not the original dataset, so why leave them connected?

It's true that the service doesn't need the original automobile price data. But it does need the schema for that data, which includes information such as how many columns there are and which columns are numeric. This schema information is necessary in order to interpret the user's data. You leave these components connected so that the scoring module will have the dataset schema when the service is running. The data isn't used, just the schema.

Hello ML_Deploy

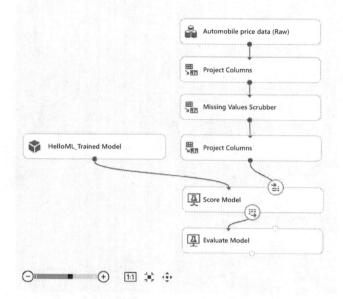

Figure 2-15. The experiment that uses the saved training model

3. Next, set your publishing input and output. To do this, follow these steps.

  a. Right-click the right input of the module named **Score Model**. Select the option **Set As Publish Input**.

  b. Right-click the output of the **Score Model** module and select **Set As Publish Output**.

After these two steps you will see two circles highlighting the chosen publish input and output on the **Score Model** module. This is shown in Figure 2-15.

4. Once you assign the publish input and output, run the experiment and then publish it into staging by clicking **Publish Web Service** at the bottom of the screen.

■ **Tip**   You can update the web service after you've published it. For example, if you want to change your model, just edit the training experiment you saved earlier, tweak the model parameters, and save the trained model (overwriting the one you saved before). When you open the scoring experiment again, you'll see a notice telling you that something has changed (that will be your trained model) and you can update the experiment. When you publish the experiment again, it will replace the web service, now using your updated model.

You can configure the service by clicking the **Configuration** tab. Here you can modify the service name (it's given the experiment name by default) and give it a description. You can also give more friendly labels for the input and output columns.

Testing the Web Service

On the **Dashboard** page, click the **Test** link under **Staging Services**. A dialog will pop up that asks you for the input data for the service. These are the same columns that appeared in the original **Automobile price data (Raw)** dataset. Enter a set of data and then click **OK**.

The results generated by the web service are displayed at the bottom of the dashboard. The way you have the service configured, the results you see are generated by the scoring module.

Moving Your Model from Staging into Production

At this point your model is now in staging, but is not yet running in production. To publish it in production you need to move it from the staging to the production environment through the following steps.

1. Configure your new web service in Azure Machine Learning Studio and make it ready for production as follows.

    a. In Azure Machine Learning Studio, click the menu called **Web Services** on the right pane. It will show a list of all your web services.

    b. Click the name of the new service you just created. You can test it by clicking the **Test** URL.

    c. Now click the configuration tab, and then select **yes** for the option **Ready For Production?** Then click the **Save** button at the bottom of the screen. Now your model is ready to be published in production.

2. Now switch to the Azure Management Portal and publish your web service into production as follows.

    a. Select **Machine Learning** on the left pane in Azure Management Portal.

    b. Choose the workspace with the experiment you want to deploy in production.

    c. Click on the name of your workspace, and then click the tab named **Web Services**.

d. Choose the **+Add** button at the bottom of the Azure Management Portal window.

Figure 2-16. *A dialog box that promotes the machine learning model from the staging server to a live production web service*

Congratulations! You have just published your very first machine learning model into production. If you click your model from the Web Services tab, you will see details such as the number of predictions made by your model over a seven-day window. The service also shows the APIs you can use to call your model as a web service either in a request/response or batch execution mode. As if this is not enough, you also get sample code you can use to invoke your new web service in C#, Python, or R. You can use this sample code to call your model as a web service from a web form in a browser or from any other application of your choice.

Accessing the Azure Machine Learning Web Service

To be useful as a web service, users need to be able to send data to the service and receive results. The web service is an Azure web service that can receive and return data in one of two ways:

- **Request/Response**: The user can send a single set of Automobile price data to the service using an HTTP protocol, and the service responds with a single result predicting the price.

- **Batch Execution**: The user can send to the service the URL of an Azure BLOB that contains one or more rows of Automobile price data. The service stores the results in another BLOB and returns the URL of that container.

On the **Dashboard** tab for the web service, there are links to information that will help a developer write code to access this service. Click the API help page link on the REQUEST/RESPONSE row and a page opens that contains sample code to use the service's request/response protocol. Similarly, the link on the BATCH EXECUTION row provides example code for making a batch request to the service.

The API help page includes samples for R, C#, and Python programming languages. For example, Listing 2-1 shows the R code that you could use to access the web service you published (the actual service URL would be displayed in your sample code).

Listing 2-1. R Code Used to Access the Service Programmatically

```
library("RCurl")
library("RJSONIO")

# Accept SSL certificates issued by public Certificate Authorities
options(RCurlOptions = list(sslVersion=3L, cainfo = system.file("CurlSSL",
"cacert.pem", package = "RCurl")))

h = basicTextGatherer()
req = list(Id="score00001",
 Instance=list(FeatureVector=list(
    "symboling"= "0",
    "make"= "0",
    "body-style"= "0",
    "wheel-base"= "0",
    "engine-size"= "0",
    "horsepower"= "0",
    "peak-rpm"= "0",
    "highway-mpg"= "0",
    "price"= "0"
 ),GlobalParameters=fromJSON('{}')))

body = toJSON(req)
api_key = "abc123" # Replace this with the API key for the web service
authz_hdr = paste('Bearer', api_key, sep=' ')

h$reset()
curlPerform(url = "https://ussouthcentral.services.azureml.net/workspaces/
fcaf778fe92f4fefb2f104acf9980a6c/services/ca2aea46a205473aabca2670c5607518/
score",
            httpheader=c('Content-Type' = "application/json",
            'Authorization' = authz_hdr),
            postfields=body,
            writefunction = h$update,
            verbose = TRUE
            )

result = h$value()
print(result)
```

Summary

In this chapter, you learned how to use Azure Machine Learning Studio to create your first experiment. You saw how to perform data preprocessing, and how to train, test, and evaluate your model in Azure Machine Learning Studio. In addition, you also saw how to deploy your new model in production. Once deployed, your machine learning model runs as a web service on Azure that can be called from a web form or any other application from a server, laptop, tablet, or smartphone. In the remainder of this book, you will learn how to use Azure Machine Learning to create experiments that solve various business problems such as customer propensity, customer churn, and predictive maintenance. In addition, you will also learn how to extend Azure Machine Learning with R scripting. Also, Chapter 4 introduces the most commonly used statistics and machine learning algorithms in Azure Machine Learning.

CHAPTER 3

■ ■ ■

Integration with R

This chapter will introduce R and show how it is integrated with Microsoft Azure Machine Learning. Through simple examples, you will learn how to write and run your own R code when working with Azure Machine Learning. You will also learn the R packages supported by Azure Machine Learning, and how you can use them in the Azure Machine Learning Studio (ML Studio).

R in a Nutshell

R is an open source statistical programming language that is commonly used by the computational statistics and data science community for solving an extensive spectrum of business problems. These problems span the following areas:

- Bioinformatics (e.g. genome analysis)

- Actuarial sciences (e.g. figuring out risk exposures for insurance, finance, and other industries)

- Telecommunication (analyzing churn in corporate and consumer customer base, fraudulent SIM card usage, or mobile usage patterns)

- Finance and banking (e.g. identifying fraud in financial transactions), manufacturing (e.g. predicting hardware component failure times), and many more.

When using R, users feel empowered by its toolbox of R packages that provides powerful capabilities for data analysis, visualization, and modeling. As of 2014, the Comprehensive R Archive Network (CRAN) provides a large collection of more than 5000 R packages. Besides CRAN, there are many other R packages available on Github (https://github.com/trending?l=r) and specialized R packages for bioinformatics in the Bioconductor R repository (www.bioconductor.org/).

■ **Note**   R was created at the University of Auckland by Joss Ihaka and Robert Gentleman in 1994. Since R's creation, many leading computer scientists and statisticians have fueled R's success by contributing to the R codebase or providing R packages that enable R users to leverage the latest techniques for statistical analysis, visualization, and data mining. This has propelled R to become one of the languages for data scientists. Learn more about R at `www.r-project.org/`.

Given the momentum in the data science community in using R to tackle machine learning problems, it is super important for a cloud-based machine learning platform to empower data scientists to continue using the familiar R scripts that they have written, and continue to be productive. Currently, more than 400 R packages are supported by Azure Machine Learning. Table 3-1 shows a subset of the R packages currently supported. These R packages enable you to model a wide spectrum of machine learning problems from market basket analysis, classification, regression, forecasting, and visualization.

Table 3-1. *R Packages Supported by Azure Machine Learning*

R packages	Description
Arules	Frequent itemsets and association rule mining
FactoMineR	Data exploration
Forecast	Univariate time series forecasts (exponential smoothing and automatic ARIMA)
ggplot2	Graphics
Glmnet	Linear regression, logistics and multinomial regression models, poisson regression, and Cox Model
Party	Tools for decision tree
randomForest	Classification and regression models based on a forest of trees
Rsonlp	General non-linear optimization using augmented lagrange multipliers
Xts	Time series
Zoo	Time series

■ Tip   To get the complete list of installed packages, create a new experiment in Cloud Machine Learning, use the **Execute R Script** module, provide the following script in the body of the **Execute R Script** module, and run the experiment. After the experiment

```
out <- data.frame(installed.packages())
maml.mapOutputPort("out")
```

completes, right-click the left output portal of the module and select **Visualize**. The packages that have been installed in Cloud Machine Learning will be listed.

Azure Machine Learning provides R language modules to enable you to integrate R into your machine learning experiments. Currently, the R language module that can be used within the Azure Machine Learning Studio (ML Studio) is the **Execute R Script** module.

The **Execute R Script** module enables you to specify input datasets (at most two datasets), an R script, and a Zip file containing a set of R scripts (optional). After the module processes the data, it produces a result dataset and an R device output. In Azure Machine Learning, the R scripts are executed using R 4.1.0.

■ Note   The R Device output shows the console output and graphics that are produced during the execution of the R script. For example, in the R script, you might have used the R plot() function. The output of plot() can be visualized when you right-click on the R Device output and choose **Visualize**.

ML Studio enables you to monitor and troubleshoot the progress of the experiment. Once the execution has completed, you can view the output log of each run of the R module. The output log will also enable you to troubleshoot issues if the execution failed.

In this chapter, you will learn how to integrate R with Azure Machine Learning. Through the use of simple examples and datasets available in ML Studio, you will gain essential skills to unleash the power of R to create exciting and useful experiments with Azure Machine Learning. Let's get started!

Building and Deploying Your First R Script

To build and deploy your first R script module, first you need to create a new experiment. After you create the experiment, you will see the **Execute R Script** module that is provided in the Azure Machine Learning Studio (ML Studio). The script will be executed by Azure Machine Learning using R 3.1.0 (the version that was installed on Cloud Machine Learning at the time of this book). Figure 3-1 shows the R Language modules.

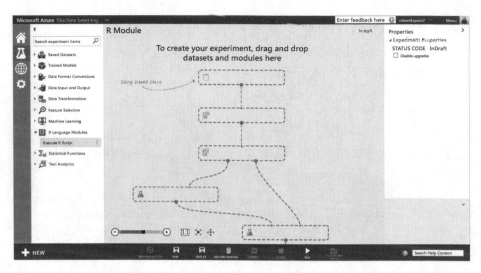

Figure 3-1. *R Language modules in ML Studio*

In this section, you will learn how to use the Execute R Script to perform sampling on a dataset. Follow these steps.

1. From the toolbox, expand the **Saved Datasets** node, and click the **Adult Census Income Binary Classification** dataset. Drag and drop it onto the experiment design area.

2. From the toolbox, expand the **R Language Modules** node, and click the **Execute R Script** module. Drag and drop it onto the experiment design area.

3. Connect the dataset to the **Execute R Script** module. Figure 3-2 shows the experiment design.

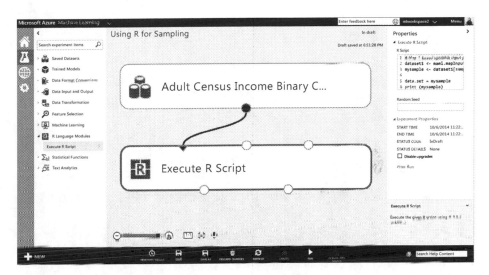

Figure 3-2. *Using the Execute R Script to perform sampling on the Adult Census Income Binary Classification dataset*

The **Execute R Script** module provides two input ports for datasets that can be used by the R script. In addition, it allows you to specify a Zip file that contains the R source script files that are used by the module. You can edit the R source script files on your local machine and test them. Then, you can compress the needed files into a Zip file and upload it to Azure Machine Learning through New > Dataset > From Local File path. After the **Execute R Script** module processes the data, the module provides two output ports: Result Dataset and an R Device. The Result Dataset corresponds to output from the R script that can be passed to the next module. The R Device output port provides you with an easy way to see the console output and graphics that are produced by the R interpreter.

Let's continue creating your first R script using ML Studio.

4. Click the **Execute R Script** module.

5. On the Properties pane, write the following R script to perform sampling:

```
# Map 1-based optional input ports to variables
dataset1 <- maml.mapInputPort(1) # class: data.frame
mysample <- dataset1[sample(1:nrow(dataset1), 50, replace=FALSE),]

data.set = mysample
print (mysample)
```

```
# Select data.frame to be sent to the output Dataset port
maml.mapOutputPort("data.set");
```

R Script to perform sampling

To use the **Execute R Script** module, the following pattern is often used:

- Map the input ports to R variables or data frame.

- Main body of the R Script.

- Map the results to the output ports (see Figure 3-3).

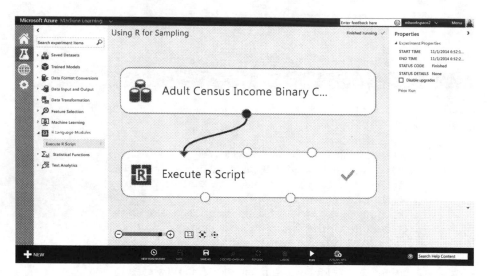

Figure 3-3. *Successful execution of the sampling experiment*

To see this pattern in action, observe that in the R script provided, the `maml.`
`mapInputPort(1)` method is used to map the dataset that was passed in from the first
input port of the module to an R data frame. Next, see the R script that is used to perform
sampling of the data. For debugging purposes, we also printed out the results of the
sample. In the last step of the R script, the results are assigned to `data.set` and mapped
to the output port using `maml.mapOutputPort("data.set")`.

You are now ready to run the experiment. To do this, click the Run icon at the bottom
pane of ML Studio. Figure 3-3 shows that the experiment has successfully completed
execution.

Once the experiment has finished running, you can see the output of the R script.
To do this, right-click on the **Result Dataset** of the **Execute R Script** module. Figure 3-4.
shows the options available when you right-click on the **Result Dataset** of the
Execute R Script module. Choose **Visualize**.

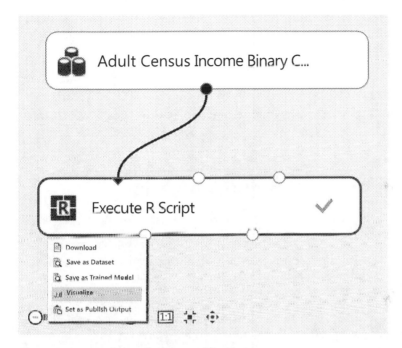

Figure 3-4. *Visualizing the output of the R script*

After you click **Visualize**, you will see that the sample consists of 50 rows. Each of the rows has 15 columns and the data distribution for the data. Figure 3-5 shows the visualization for the Result dataset.

Using R for Sampling › Execute R Script › Result Dataset ⊗

rows	**columns**							
50	15							
	age	workclass	fnlwgt	education	education-num	marital-status	occupation	relationship
view as								
59	Private	106748	7th-8th	4	Married-civ-spouse	Other-service	Wife	
68	Without-pay	174695	Some-college	10	Married-spouse-absent	Farming-fishing	Unmarried	
25	Private	159732	Some-college	10	Never-married	Adm-clerical	Not-in-family	
59		254765	Some-college	10	Married-civ-spouse		Husband	
46	Private	294907	5th-6th	3	Married-civ-spouse	Machine-op-inspct	Husband	
50	Private	200618	Assoc-acdm	12	Divorced	Craft-repair	Not-in-family	
32	Private	158291	HS-grad	9	Married-civ-	Craft-repair	Husband	

Statistics

Visualizations

To create a graph, select a column in the table

Figure 3-5. *Visualization of result dataset produced by the R script*

Congratulations, you have just successfully completed the integration of your first simple R script in Azure Machine Learning! In the next section, you will learn how to use Azure Machine Learning and R to create a machine learning model.

▓ **Note** Learn more about R and Machine Learning at http://ocw.mit.edu/courses/ sloan-school-of-management/15-097-prediction-machine-learning-and-statistics- spring-2012/lecture-notes/MIT15_097S12_lec02.pdf.

Using R for Data Preprocessing

In many machine learning tasks, dimensionality reduction is an important step that is used to reduce the number of features for the machine learning algorithm. Principal component analysis (PCA) is a commonly used dimensionality reduction technique. PCA reduces the dimensionality of the dataset by finding a new set of variables (principal components) that are linear combinations of the original dataset, and are uncorrelated with all other variables. In this section, you will learn how to use R for preprocessing the data and reducing the dimensionality of dataset.

Let's get started with using the **Execute R Script** module to perform principal component analysis of one of the sample datasets available in ML Studio. Follow these steps.

1.   Create a new experiment.

2.   From Saved Datasets, choose **CRM Dataset Shared** (see Figure 3-6).

Figure 3-6. *Using the sample dataset, CRM Dataset Shared*

3. Right-click the output node, and choose **Visualize**. From the visualization shown in Figure 3-7, you will see that are 230 columns.

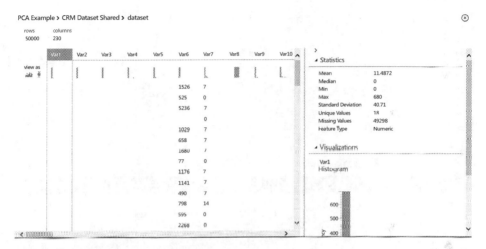

Figure 3-7. Initial 230 columns from the CRM Shared dataset

4. Before you perform PCA, you need to make sure that the inputs to the **Execute R Script** module are numeric. For the sample dataset of CRM Dataset Shared, you know that the first 190 columns are numeric, and the remaining 40 columns are categorical. You first use the **Project Columns**, and set the **Selected Column | column indices** to be 1-190.

5. Next, use the **Missing Values Scrubber** module to replace the missing value with 0, as follows:

   a. For missing values: Custom substitution value

   b. Replace with Value: 0

   c. Cols with all MV: KeepColumns

   d. MV indicator column: DoNotGenerate

6. Once the missing values have been scrubbed, use the **Metadata Editor** module to change the data type for all the columns to be Integer.

7. Next, drag and drop the **Execute R Script** module to the design surface and connect the modules, as shown in Figure 3-8.

Figure 3-8. *Using the Execute R Script module to perform PCA*

8. Click the **Execute R Script** module. You can provide the following script that will be used to perform PCA:

```
# Map 1-based optional input ports to variables
dataset1 <- maml.mapInputPort(1)
# Perform PCA on the first 190 columns
pca = prcomp(dataset1[,1:190])

# Return the top 10 principal components
top_pca_scores = data.frame(pca$x[,1:10])
data.set = top_pca_scores
plot(data.set)
# Select data.frame to be sent to the output Dataset port
maml.mapOutputPort("data.set");
```

Figure 3-9 shows how to use the script in ML Studio.

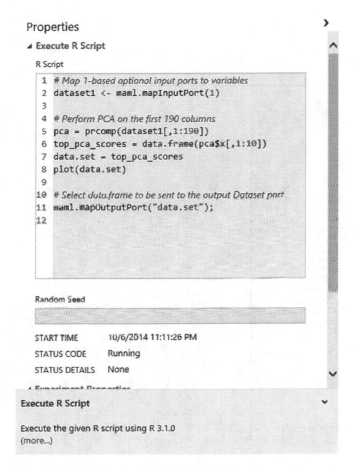

Figure 3-9. *Performing PCA on the first 190 columns*

9. Click **Run**.

10. Once the experiment has successfully executed, click the **Result dataset** node of the **Execute R Script** module. Click **Visualize**.

11. Figure 3-10 shows the top ten principal components for the CRM Shared dataset. The principal components are used in the subsequent steps for building the classification model.

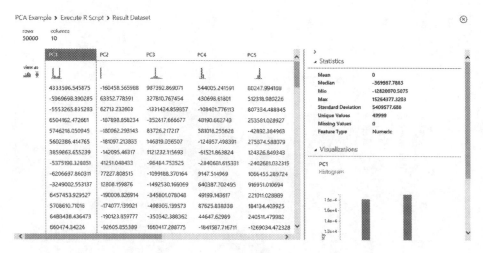

Figure 3-10. *Principal components identified for the CRM Shared dataset*

■ **Tip** You can also provide a script bundle containing the R script in a Zip file, and use it in the **Execute R Script** module.

Using a Script Bundle (Zip)

If you have an R script that you have been using and want to use it as part of the experiment, you can Zip up the R script, and upload it to ML Studio as a dataset. To use a script bundle with the **Execute R Script** module, you will first need to package up the file in Zip format, so follow these steps.

1. Navigate to the folder containing the R scripts that you intend to use in your experiment (see Figure 3-11).

Figure 3-11. *Folder containing the R script pcaexample.r*

2. Select all the files that you want to package up and right-click. In this example, right-click the file **pcaexample.r**, and choose **Send to Compressed (zipped) folder**, as shown in Figure 3-12.

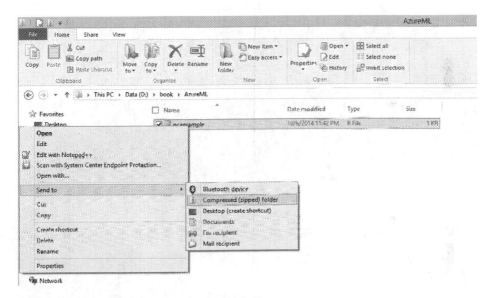

Figure 3-12. *Packaging the R scripts as a ZIP file*

3. Next, upload the zip file to ML Studio. TO do this, choose **New DATASET ➤ From Local File**. Select the Zip file that you want to upload, as shown in Figures 3-13 and 3-14.

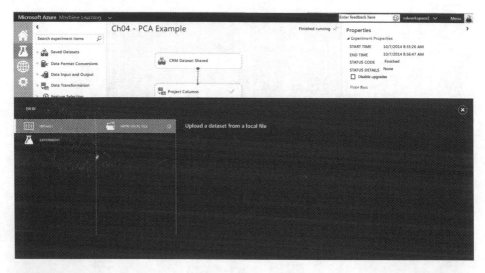

Figure 3-13. *New Dataset ➤ From Local File*

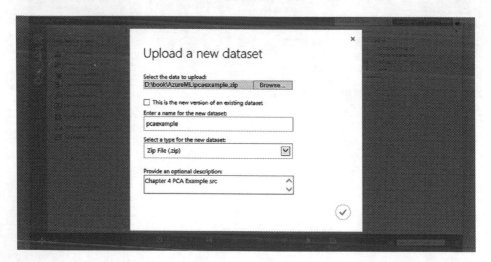

Figure 3-14. *Uploading a new dataset*

4. Once the dataset has been uploaded, you can use it in your experiment. To do this, from **Saved Datasets**, select the **uploaded Zip file**, and drag and drop it to the experiment.

5. Connect the uploaded Zip file to the **Execute R Script** module – **Script Bundle (Zip)** input, as shown in Figure 3-15.

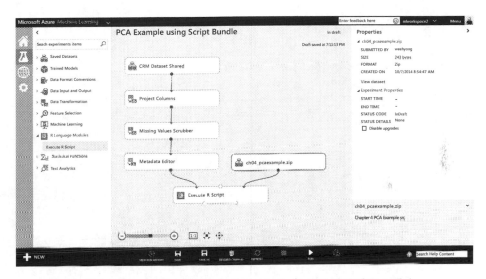

Figure 3-15. *Using the script bundle as an input to the Execute R Script module*

6. In the **Execute R Script** module, specify where the R script
    can be found, as follows and as shown in Figure 3-16:

```
# Map 1-based optional input ports to variables
dataset1 <- maml.mapInputPort(1)
# Contents of optional Zip port are in ./src/
source("src/pcaexample.r");

# Select data.frame to be sent to the output Dataset port
maml.mapOutputPort("data.set");
```

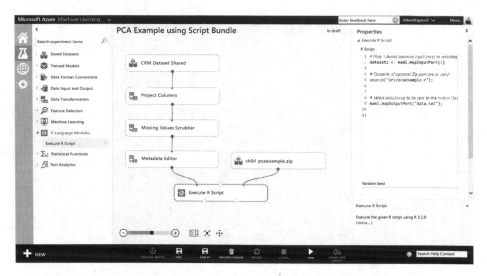

Figure 3-16. *Using the script bundle as inputs to the Execute R Script module*

7.   You are now ready to run the experiment using the R script in the Zip file that you have uploaded to ML Studio. Using the script bundle allows you to easily reference an R script file that you can test outside of ML Studio. In order to update the script, you will have to re-upload the Zip file.

Building and Deploying a Decision Tree Using R

In this section, you will learn how to use R to build a machine learning model. When using R, you can tap into the large collection of R packages that implement various machine learning algorithms for classification, clustering, regression, K-Nearest Neighbor, market basket analysis, and much more.

▦ **Note**   When you use the machine learning algorithms available in R and execute them using the **Execute R** module, you can only visualize the model and parameters. You cannot save the trained model and use it as input to other ML Studio modules.

Using ML studio, several R machine learning algorithms are provided. For example, you can use the **R Auto-ARIMA** module to build an optimal autoregressive moving average model for a univariate time series. You can also use the **R K-Nearest Neighbor Classification** module to create a k-nearest neighbor (KNN) classification model.

In this section, you will learn how to use an R package called **rpart** to build a decision tree. The **rpart** package provides you with recursive partitioning algorithms for performing classification and regression.

▓ **Note**   Learn more about the **rpart** R package at http://cran.r-project.org/web/packages/rpart/rpart.pdf.

For this exercise, you will use the Adult Census Income Binary Classification dataset. Let's get started.

1.   From the toolbox, drag and drop the following modules on the experiment design area:

   a.   **Adult Census Income Binary Classification** dataset (available under **Saved Datasets**)

   b.   **Project Columns** (available from **Data Transformation ➤ Manipulation**)

   c.   **Execute R Script** module (found under **R Language** modules)

2.   Connect the **Adult Census Income Binary Classification** dataset to **Project Columns**.

3.   Click **Project Columns** to select the columns that will be used in the experiment. Select the following columns: age, sex, education, income, marital-status, occupation.

   Figure 3-17 shows the selection of the columns and Figure 3-18 shows the completed experiment and the Project Columns properties.

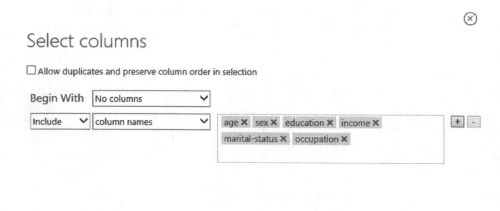

Figure 3-17. Selecting columns that will be used

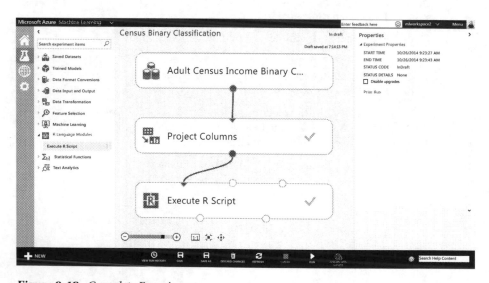

Figure 3-18. Complete Experiment

4. Connect the **Project Columns** to **Execute R Script**.

5. Click **Execute R Script** and provide the following script. Figure 3-19 shows the R script in ML studio.

```
library(rpart)

# Map 1-based optional input ports to variables
Dataset1 <- maml.mapInputPort(1) # class: data.frame
```

```
        fit <- rpart(income ~ age + sex + education + occupation,
method="class", data=Dataset1)

        # display the results, and summary of the splits
        printcp(fit)
        plotcp(fit)
        summary(fit)

        # plot the decision tree
        plot(fit, uniform=TRUE, margin = 0.1,compress = TRUE,
main="Classification Tree for Census Dataset")
        text(fit, use.n=TRUE, all=TRUE, cex=0.8, pretty=1)

        data.set = Dataset1

        # select data.frame to be sent to the output Dataset port
        maml.mapOutputPort("data.set");
```

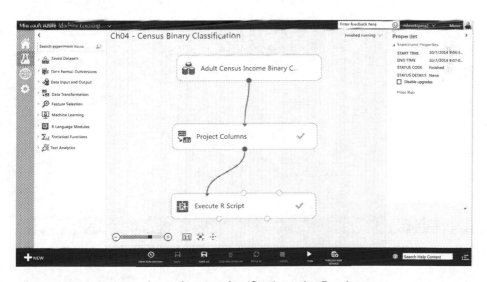

Figure 3-19. *Experiment for performing classification using R script*

In the R script, first load the `rpart` library using `library()`. Next, map the dataset that is passed to the **Execute R Script** module to a data frame.

To build the decision tree, you will use the `rpart` function. Several type of methods are supported by rpart: `class` (classification), and `anova` (regression). In this exercise, you will use `rpart` to perform classification (i.e. `method="class"`), as follows:

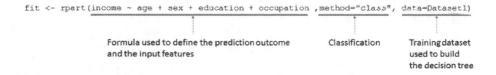

```
fit <- rpart(income ~ age + sex + education + occupation ,method="class", data=Dataset1)
```

Formula used to define the prediction outcome
and the input features   Classification   Training dataset
                                                        used to build
                                                        the decision tree

The formula specified uses the format: predictionVariable ~ inputfeature1 +
inputfeature2 + ...

After the decision tree has been constructed, the R script invokes the printcp(),
plotcp(), and summary() functions to display the results, and a summary of each of the
split values in the tree. In the R script, the plot() function is used to plot the rpart model.
By default, when the rpart model is plotted, an abbreviated representation is used to
denote the split value. In the R script, the setting of pretty=1 is added to enable the actual
split values to be shown (see Figure 3-20).

Figure 3-20. *The R script in ML Studio*

You are now ready to run the experiment. To do this, click the Run icon at the bottom
pane of ML Studio. Once the experiment has executed successfully, you can view the
details of the decision tree and also visualize the overall shape of the decision tree.

To view the details of the decision tree, click the **Execute R Script** module and **View
output log** (shown in Figure 3-21) in the **Properties** pane.

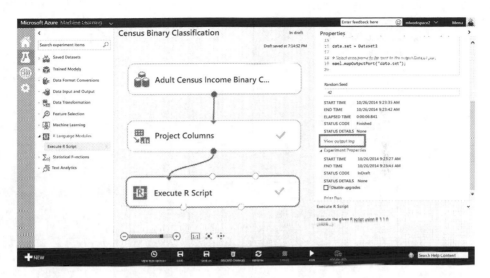

Figure 3-21. *View output log for Execute R Script*

A sample of the output log is shown:

```
[ModuleOutput] Classification tree:
[ModuleOutput]
[ModuleOutput]
[ModuleOutput]
[ModuleOutput] Variables actually used in tree construction:
[ModuleOutput]
[ModuleOutput] [1] age        education  occupation sex
[ModuleOutput]
[ModuleOutput]
...
[ModuleOutput]    Primary splits:
[ModuleOutput]
[ModuleOutput]        education  splits as  LLLLLLLLLRRLRLRL,
                      improve=1274.3680, (0 missing)
[ModuleOutput]
[ModuleOutput]        occupation splits as  LLLRLLLLLRRLLL,
                      improve=1065.9400, (1843 missing)
[ModuleOutput]
[ModuleOutput]        age        < 29.5 to the left,  improve= 980.1513, (0
                      missing)
[ModuleOutput]
[ModuleOutput]        sex        splits as  LR, improve= 555.3667, (0
                      missing)
```

To visualize the decision tree, click the **R Device** output port (i.e. the second output of the **Execute R Script** module), and you will see the decision tree that you just constructed using rpart (shown in Figure 3-22).

Classification Tree for Census Dataset

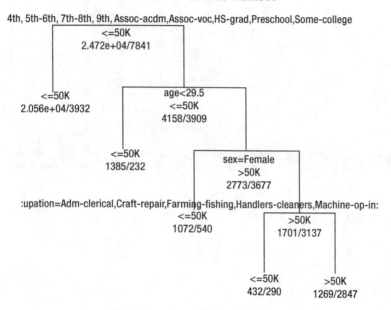

Figure 3-22. *Decision tree constructed using rpart*

■ **Note**   Azure Machine Learning provides a good collection of saved datasets that can be used in your experiments. In addition, you can also find an extensive collection of datasets at the UCI Machine Learning Repository at http://archive.ics.uci.edu/ml/datasets.html.

Summary

In this chapter, you learned about the exciting possibilities offered by R integration with Azure Machine Learning. You learned how to use the different R Language Modules in ML Studio. As you designed your experiment using R, you learned how to map the inputs and outputs of the module to R variables and data frames. Next, you learned how to build your first R script to perform data sampling and how to visualize the results using the built-in data visualization tools available in ML Studio. With that as foundation, you moved on to building and deploying experiments that use R for data preprocessing through an R Script bundle and building decision trees.

## PART 2

Statistical and Machine Learning Algorithms

CHAPTER 4

■ ■ ■

Introduction to Statistical and Machine Learning Algorithms

This chapter will serve as a reference for some of the most commonly used algorithms in Microsoft Azure Machine Learning. We will provide a brief introduction to algorithms such as linear and logistic regression, k-means for clustering, decision trees, decision forests (random forests, boosted decision trees, and Gemini), neural networks, support vector machines, and Bayes point machines.

This chapter will provide a good foundation and reference material for some of the algorithms you will encounter in the rest of the book. We group these algorithms into the following categories:

- Regression

- Classification

- Clustering

Regression Algorithms

Let's first talk about the commonly used regression techniques in the Azure Machine Learning service. Regression techniques are used to predict response variables with numerical outcomes, such as predicting the miles per gallon of a car or predicting the temperature of a city. The input variables may be numeric or categorical. However, what is common with these algorithms is that the output (or response variable) is numeric. We'll review some of the most commonly used regression techniques including linear regression, neural networks, decision trees, and boosted decision tree regression.

Linear Regression

Linear regression is one of the oldest prediction techniques in statistics. In fact, it traces its roots back to the work of Carl Friedrich Gauss in 1795. The goal of linear regression is to fit a linear model between the response and independent variables, and use it to predict the outcome given a set of observed independent variables. A simple linear regression model is a formula with the structure of

$$Y = \beta_0 + \beta_1 X_1 + \beta_2 X_2 + \beta_3 X_3 + \beta_4 X_4 + \cdots + \varepsilon$$

where

- Y is the response variable (i.e. the outcome you are trying to predict) such as miles per gallon.

- X_1, X_2, X_3, etc. are the independent variables used to predict the outcome.

- β_0 is a constant that is the intercept of the regression line.

- $\beta_1, \beta_2, \beta_3$, etc. are the coefficients of the independent variables. These refer to the partial slopes of each variable.

- ε is the error or noise associated with the response variable that cannot be explained by the independent variables X1, X2, and X3.

A linear regression model has two components: a deterministic portion (i.e. $b_1 X_1 + b_2 X_2 + \ldots$) and a random portion (i.e. the error, ε). You can think of these two components as the signal and noise in the model.

If you only have one input variable, X, the regression model is the best line that fits the data. Figure 4-1 shows an example of a simple linear regression model that predicts a car's miles per gallon from its horsepower. With two input variables, the linear regression is the best plane that fits a set of data points in a 3D space. The coefficients of the variables (i.e. $\beta_1, \beta_2, \beta_3$, etc.) are the partial slopes of each variable. If you hold all other variables constant, then the outcome Y will increase by β_1 when the variable X_1 increases by 1. This is why economists typically use the phrase "*ceteris paribus*"" or "*all other things being equal*" to describe the effect of one independent variable on a given outcome.

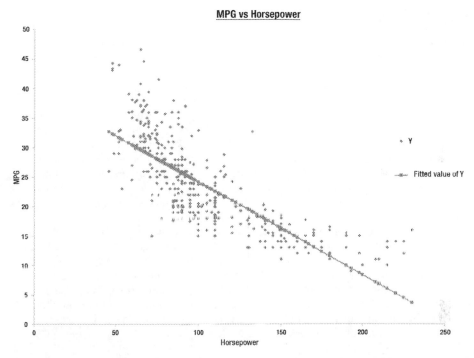

Figure 4-1. *A simple linear regression model that predicts a car's miles per gallon from its horsepower*

Linear regression uses the least squares or gradient descent methods to find the best model coefficients for a given dataset. The least squares method achieves this by minimizing the sum of the squared error between the fitted and actual values of each observation in the training data. The gradient descent finds the optimal model coefficients by updating the coefficients in each iteration. The updates go in the direction so that the sum of errors between the model fitted and the actual values of the training data are reduced. Through several iterations it finds the local minimum by moving in the direction of the negative gradient, hence the name.

▨ **Note**   You can learn more about linear regression from the book *Business Analysis Using Regression: A Casebook* (Foster, D. P., Stine, R.H., Waterman, R.P.; New York, USA; Springer-Verlag, 1998).

Neural Networks

Artificial neural networks are a set of algorithms that mimic the functioning of the brain. There are many different neural network algorithms, including backpropagation networks, Hopfield networks, Kohonen networks (also known as self-organizing maps), and adaptive resonance theory (or ART) networks. However, the most common is the back-propagation algorithm, also known as multilayered perceptron.

The back-propagation network has several neurons arranged in layers. The most commonly used architecture is the three-layered network shown in Figure 4-2. This architecture has one input, one hidden, and one output layer. However, you can also have two or more hidden layers. The number of input and output nodes are determined by the dataset. Basically, the number of input nodes equals the number of independent variables you want to use to predict the output. The number of output nodes is the same as the number of response variables. In contrast, the number of hidden nodes is more flexible.

The development of neural network models is done in two steps: training and testing. During training, you show the neural network a set of examples from the training set. Each example has values of the independent as well as the response variables. During training, you show the examples several times to the neural network. At each iteration, the network predicts the response. In the forward propagation phase of training, each node in the hidden and output layers calculates a weighted sum of its inputs, and then uses this sum to compute its output through an activate function. The output of each neuron in the neural network usually uses the following sigmoidal activate function:

$$f(x) = \frac{1}{1+e^{-x}}$$

There are, however, other activation functions that can be used in neural networks, such as Gaussian, hyperbolic tangent (tanh), linear threshold, and even a simple linear function.

Let's assume there are M input nodes. The connection weights between the input nodes and the first hidden layer are denoted by w^1_{ij}.

At each hidden node the weighted sum is given by

$$S_j = \sum_{i=0}^{M-1} (a_i w^1_{ij})$$

When the weighted sum is calculated, the sigmoidal activate function is calculated as follows:

$$f(S_j) = \frac{1}{1+e^{-S_j}}$$

After the activation level of the output node is calculated, the backward propagation step starts. In this phase, the algorithm calculates the error of its prediction based on the actual response value. Using the gradient descent method, it adjusts the weights of all connections in proportion the error. The weights are adjusted in a way that reduces the error the next time. After several iterations, the neural network converges to a solution.

During testing, you simply use the trained model to score records. For each record, the neural network predicts the value of the response for a given set of input variables (see Figure 4-2).

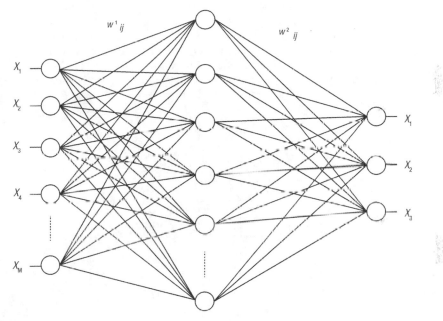

Figure 4-2. *A neural network with three layers: one input, one hidden, and one output layer*

The learning rate determines the rate of convergence to a solution. If the learning rate is too low, the algorithm will need more learning iterations (and hence more time) to converge to the minimum. In contrast, if the learning rate is too large, the algorithm bounces around and may never find the local minimum. Hence the neural net will be a poor predictor.

Another important parameter is the number of hidden nodes. The accuracy of the neural network may increase with the number of hidden nodes. However, this increases the processing time and can lead to over-fitting. In general, increasing the number of hidden nodes or hidden layers can easily lead to over-parameterization, which will increase the risk of over-fitting. One rule of thumb is to start with the number of hidden nodes equal roughly to the square root of the number of input nodes. Another general rule of thumb is that the number of neurons in the hidden layer should be between the size of the input layer and the size of the output layer. For example, (Number of input nodes + number of output nodes) x 2/3. These rules of thumb are merely starting points, intended to avoid over-fitting; the optimal number can only be found through experimentation and validation of performance on test data.

Decision Trees

Decision tree algorithms are hierarchical techniques that work by splitting the dataset iteratively based on certain statistical criteria. The goal of decision trees is to maximize the variance across different nodes in the tree, and minimize the variance within each node. Figure 4-3 shows a simple decision tree created with two splits of the data. The root node (Node 0) contains all the data in the dataset. The algorithm splits the data based on a defined statistic, creating three new nodes (Node 1, Node 2, and Node 3). Using the same statistic, it splits the data again at Node 1, creating two more leaf nodes (i.e. Nodes 4 and 5). The decision tree makes its prediction for each data row by traversing to the leaf nodes (i.e. one of the terminal nodes: Node 2, 3, 4, or 5).

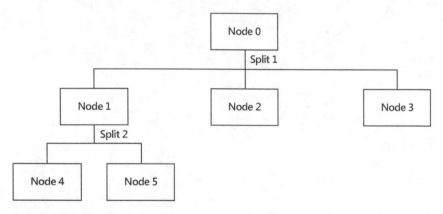

Figure 4-3. *A simple decision tree with two data splits*

Figure 4-4 shows a fictional example of a very simple decision tree that predicts whether a customer will buy a bike or not. In this example, the original dataset has 100 examples. The most predictive variable is age, so the decision first splits the data by age. Customers younger than 30 fall in the left branch while those aged 30 or above fall in the right branch. The next most important variable is gender, so in the next level the decision tree splits the data by gender. In the younger branch (i.e. for customer customers under 30), the decision tree splits the data into male and female branches. It also does the same for the older branch. Finally, Figure 4-4 shows the number of examples in each node and the probability to purchase. As a result, if you have a female customer aged 23, the tree predicts that she only has a 30% chance of buying the bike because she will end up in Node 3. A male customer aged 45 will have an 80% chance of buying a bike since he will end up in Node 6 in the tree.

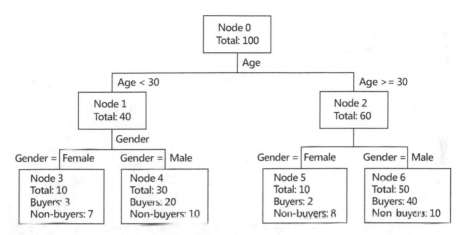

Figure 4-4. A simple decision tree to predict likelihood to buy bikes

Some of the most commonly used decision tree algorithms include Iterative Dichotomizer 3 (ID3), C4.5 and C5.0 (successors of ID3), Automatic Interaction Detection (AID), Chi Squared Automatic Interaction Detection (CHAID), and Classification and Regression Tree (CART). While very useful, the ID3, C4.5, C5.0, and CHAID algorithms are classification algorithms and are not useful for regression. As the name suggests, the CART algorithm can be used for either classification or regression.

How do you choose the variable to use for splitting data at each level? Each decision tree algorithm uses a different statistic to choose the best variable for splitting. ID3, C4.5, and C5.0 use information gain, while CART uses a metric called Gini impurity. Gini impurity measures the misclassification rate of a randomly chosen example.

■ **Note** More information on decision trees is available in the book *Data Mining and Market Intelligence for Optimal Market Returns* by S. Chiu and D. Tavella (Oxford, UK, Butterworth-Heinemann, 2008) and at http://en.wikipedia.org/wiki/Decision_tree_learning.

Boosted Decision Trees

Boosted decision trees are a form of ensemble models. Like other ensemble models, boosted decision trees use several decision trees to produce superior predictors. Each of the individual decision trees can be weak predictors. However, when combined they produce superior results.

As discussed in Chapter 1, there are three key steps to building an ensemble model: a) data selection, b) training classifiers, and c) combining classifiers.

The first step to build an ensemble model is data selection for the classifier models. When sampling the data, a key goal is to maximize diversity of the models, since this improves the accuracy of the solution. In general, the more diverse your models, the better the performance of your final classifier, and the smaller the variance of its predictions.

Step 2 of the process entails training several individual classifiers. But how do you assign the classifiers? Of the many available strategies, the two most popular are bagging and boosting. The bagging algorithm uses different random subsets of the data to train each model. The models can then be trained in parallel over their random subset of training data. In contrast, the boosting algorithm improves overall performance by sequentially training the models, testing the performance of each on the training data. The examples in the training set that were misclassified are given more importance in subsequent training. Thus, during training, each additional model focuses more on the misclassified data. The boosted decision tree algorithm uses the boosting strategy. In this case, every new decision tree is trained with emphasis on the misclassified cases to reduce the error rates. This is how a boosted decision tree produces superior results from weak decision trees.

It is important to watch two key parameters of the boosted decision tree: the number of leaves in each decision tree and the number of boosting iterations. The number of leaves in each tree determines the amount of interaction allowed between variables in the model. If this number is set to 2, then no interaction is allowed. If it is set to 3, the model can include effects of interaction of at most two variables. You need to try different values to find the one that works best for your dataset. It has been reported that 4-8 leaves per tree yields good results for most applications. In contrast, having only two leaves per tree leads to poor results. The second important parameter to tweak is the number of boosting iterations (i.e. the number of trees in the model). A very large number of trees reduces the errors, but easily leads to over-fitting. To avoid over-fitting, you need to find an optimal number of trees that minimizes the error on a validation dataset.

Finally, once you train all the classifiers, the final step is to combine their results to make a final prediction. There are several approaches to combining the outcomes, ranging from a simple majority to a weighted majority voting.

■ **Note**   You can learn more about boosted decision trees from the book *Ensemble Machine Learning, methods and applications* by C. Zhang and Y. Ma (New York, NY: pp. 1 - 34, Springer, 2012) and at http://en.wikipedia.org/wiki/Gradient_boosting#Gradient_tree_boosting.

Classification Algorithms

Classification is a type of supervised machine learning. In supervised learning, the goal is to infer a function using labeled training data. The function can then be used to determine the label for a new dataset (where the labels are unknown). A non-exhaustive list of classification algorithms that can be used for building the model includes decision trees, logistic regression, neural networks, support vector machines, naïve Bayes, and Bayes point machines.

Classification algorithms are used to predict the label for input data (where the label is unknown). Labels are also referred to as classes, groups, or target variables. For example, a telecommunication company wants to predict the following:

- *Churn*: Customers who have an inclination to switch to a different telecommunication provider

- *Propensity to Buy*: Customers willing to buy new products or services

- *Up-selling*: Customers willing to buy upgraded services or add-ons

To achieve this, the telecommunication company builds a classification model using training data (where the labels are known or have already been predefined). In this section, you'll look at several common classification algorithms that can be used for building the model. Once the model has been built and validated using test data, data scientists at the telecommunication company can use the model to predict churn, propensity to buy, and up-selling labels for customers (where the labels are unknown). Consequently, the telecommunication company can use these predictions to design marketing strategies that can reduce the customer churn and offer services to the customers that are more willing to buy new services or up-sell.

Other scenarios where classification algorithms are commonly used include financial institutions, where models are used to determine whether a credit card transaction is a fraudulent case or if a loan application should be approved based on the financial profile of the customer. Hotels and airlines use models to determine whether a customer should be upgraded to a higher level of service (e.g. from economy to business class, from a normal room to a suite, etc.).

The classification problem is defined as follows: given an input sample of $X = (x_1, x_2, ... x_d)$, where x_i refers to an item in the sample of size d. The goal of classification is to learn the mapping $X \rightarrow Y$, where $y \in Y$ is a class.

An instance of data belongs to one of J groups (or classes), such as $C_1, C_2, ..., C_j$. For example, in a two-class classification problem for the telecommunication scenario, Class C_1 refers to customers that will churn and switch to a new telecommunication provider, and Class C_2 refers to customers that will not churn.

To achieve this, labeled training data is first used to train a model using one of the classification algorithms. This is then validated by using test data to determine the number of mistakes made by the trained model (i.e. the classifier). Various metrics are used to measure the performance of the classifier. These include measuring the accuracy, precision, recall, and the area under curve (AUC) of the trained model.

In the earlier sections, you learned how decision trees, boosted decision trees and neural networks work. These algorithms are useful for both regression and classification. In this section, you will learn how support vector machines and Bayes point machines work.

Support Vector Machines

Support vector machines (SVMs) were introduced by Bernhard E. Boser, Isabelle Guyon, and Vladimir N. Vapnik at the Conference on Learning Theory (COLOT) IN 1992. A SVM is based on techniques grounded in statistical learning theory, and is considered a type of kernel-based learning algorithm.

The core idea of SVMs is to find the separating hyperplane that separates the training data into two classes, with a gap (or margin) that is as wide as possible. When there are only two input variables, a straight line separates the data into two classes. In higher-dimensional space (i.e. more than two input variables), a hyperplane separates the training data into two classes. Figure 4-5 shows how a hyperplane separates the two classes, and the margin. The circled items are the support vectors because they define the optimal hyperplane, which provides the maximum margin.

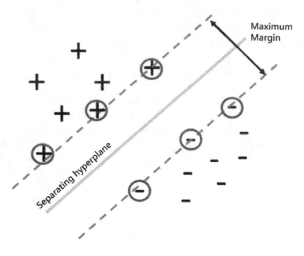

Figure 4-5. Support vector machine, separating hyperplane and margin

Consider the following example. Suppose a telecommunication company has the following training data consisting of n customers. Out of these n customers, let's assume that 50 customers will churn, and the other 50 customers will not. For each customer, you extract 10 input variables (or features) that will be used to represent the customer. Given a customer who has used the service for some time, the data scientist and business analysts in the telecommunication company want to determine whether this customer will churn and move to a different telecommunication provider.

Suppose the training data consists of the following: $(x_1, y_1), \ldots, (x_n, y_n)$, where (x_i, y_j) denotes to x_i mapped to the class y_j. The hyperplane decision function is

$$D(x) = (w \cdot x) + w_0$$

where w and w_0 are coefficients. A separating hyperplane will satisfy the following constraints:

$$(w \cdot x) + w_0 \geq +1 \quad if \quad y_i = +1$$

$$(w \cdot x) + w_0 \leq -1 \quad if \quad y_i = -1, \quad i = 1,\ldots,n$$

An optimal separating hyperplane is one that enables the maximum margin between the two classes. These two constraints for describing the hyperplane can be represented using the equation

$$y_i[(w \cdot x) + w_0] \geq 1 \quad where \quad i = 1,\ldots,n.$$

This equation can be used for representing all hyperplanes that can be used for separating the data. Often, the equation is not solved directly in its current form (also referred to as the primal form), due to the difficulty in directly computing the value of the norm of $\|w\|$. In practice, the dual form of the equation is used for solving the optimization problem that will identify the optimal hyperplane.

■ **Note** You can learn more about support vector machines and how the margin can be maximized from the following book:

Vladimir, C. and Filip, M., *Learning From Data (Concepts, Theory and Methods).* pp. 353 – 384 (Wiley-Interscience, 1998).

A good overview of support vector machines can be found at http://en.wikipedia.org/wiki/Support_vector_machine.

Azure Machine Learning provides a **Two-Class Support Vector Machine** module, which enables you to build a model that supports binary predictions. The inputs to the module can be either continuous and/or categorical variables. The module provides several parameters that can be used to fine-tune the behavior of the support vector machine algorithm. These include

- *Number of iterations*: Determines the speed of training the model. This parameter enables you to balance between training speed and model accuracy. The default value is set to 1.

- *Lambda*: Weight for L1 regularization used for tuning the complexity of the model that is produced. The default value of Lambda is set to 0.001. A non-zero value is used to avoid over-fitting the model.

- *Normalize features*: Determines whether the algorithm normalizes the values.

- *Project to unit-sphere*: Determines whether the algorithm projects the values to a unit-sphere.

- *Random Number Seed*: The seed value used for random number generation when computing the model.

- *Allow unknown categorical levels*: Determines whether the algorithm supports unknown categorical values. If this is set to True, the algorithm creates an additional level for each categorical column. The additional level is used for mapping levels in the test dataset that are not found in the training dataset.

Bayes Point Machines

Bayes point machines (BPMs) are a type of linear classification algorithm that was introduced by Ralf Herbrich, Thore Grapel, and Colin Campbell in 2001. The core idea of the Bayes point machine algorithm is to identify an "average" classifier that is able to effectively and efficiently approximate the theoretical optimal Bayesian average of several linear classifiers (based on their ability to generalize). The "average" classifier is known as the Bayes point. In empirical studies, Bayes point machines have consistently outperformed support vector machines for both lab and real-world data.

■ **Note**   The Bayes point machine algorithm used in Azure Machine Learning is based on Infer.Net and provides improvements to the original Bayes point machine algorithm. These improvements enable the Bayes point machine used in Azure Machine Learning to be more robust and less prone to over-fitting of the data. It also reduces the need to perform performance tunings.

Some of these improvements include the use of expectation propagation as the message-passing algorithm. In addition, the implementation does not require the use of parameter sweeping and having normalized data.

Recall the earlier definition of the classification problem: given an input sample $X = (x_1, x_2, \cdots, x_d)$, where x_i refer to an item in the sample of size d. The goal of classification is to learn the mapping $X \rightarrow Y$, where $y \in Y$ is a class.

Given an item in the sample x_i, where x_i is a vector with one or more variables. The BPM figures out the class label for x_i by performing the following steps:

- Computing the inner product of x_i with a weight vector w.

- Determining whether x_i belongs to a class y, if $(x_i \cdot w)$ is positive. $(x_i \cdot w$ is the inner product of the vectors x_i and w). Gaussian noise is added to the computation.

During training, the BPM algorithm learns the posterior distribution for w using a prior and the training data. The Gaussian noise used in the computation helps to address cases where there is no w that can perfectly classify the training data (i.e. when the two classes in the training data are not linearly separable).

■ **Note** You can learn more about BPMs at `http://research.microsoft.com/apps/` `pubs/default.aspx?id=65611`.

In addition, the following tutorial for using Infer.Net and BPMs provides insights into how the algorithm works:

`http://research.microsoft.com/en-us/um/cambridge/projects/infernet/docs/` `Bayes%20Point%20Machine%20tutorial.aspx`.

Azure Machine Learning provides a **Two-Class Bayes Point Machine** module, which enables you to build a model that supports binary predictions. The module provides several parameters that can be used to fine-tune the behavior of the **Bayes Point Machine** module. These include

- *Number of training iterations*: Determines the number of iterations used by the message-passing algorithm in training. Generally, the expectation is that more iterations improve the accuracy of the predictions made by the model. The default number of training iterations is 30.

- *Include bias*: Determines whether a constant bias value is added to each training and prediction instance.

Similar to the **Support Vector Machine** Module, the parameter called **Allow unknown categorical levels** is supported.

Clustering Algorithms

Clustering is a type of unsupervised machine learning. In clustering, the goal is to group similar objects together. Most existing cluster algorithms can be categorized as follows:

- *Partitioning*: Divide a data set into k partitions of data. Each partition corresponds to a cluster.

- *Hierarchical*: Given a data set, hierarchical approaches start either bottom-up or top-down when constructing the clusters. In the bottom-up approach (also known as agglomerative approach), the algorithm starts with each item in the data set assigned to one cluster. As the algorithm moves up the hierarchy, it merges the individual clusters (that are similar) into bigger clusters. This continues until all the clusters have been merged into one (root of the hierarchy). In the top-down approach (also known as divisive approach), the algorithm starts with all the items in one cluster, and in each iteration, divides into smaller clusters.

- *Density*: Density-based algorithms grow clusters by considering the density (number of items) in the "neighborhood" of each item. They are often used for identifying clusters that have "arbitrary" shapes. In contrast, most partitioning-based algorithms rely on the use of a distance measure. This produces clusters that have regular shapes (e.g. spherical).

▧ **Note**   Read a good overview of various clustering algorithms at `http://en.wikipedia.org/wiki/Cluster_analysis`.

In this chapter, we will focus on partitioning-based clustering algorithms. Specifically, you will learn how k-means clustering works.

For partitioning-based cluster algorithms, it is important to be able to measure the distance (or similarity) between points and vectors. Various distance measures include Euclidean, Cosine, Manhattan (also known as City-block) distance, Chebychev, Minkowski, and Mahalanobis distance.

In Azure Machine Learning, the **K-Means Clustering** module supports Euclidean and Cosine distance measures. Given two points, p1 and p2, the Euclidean distance between p1 and p2 is the length of the line segment that connects the two points. The Euclidean distance can also be used to measure the distance between two vectors. Given two vectors, v1 and v2, the Cosine distance is the cosine of the angle between v1 and v2.

The distance measure used for clustering is chosen based on the type of data being clustered. Euclidean distance is sensitive to the scale/magnitude of the vectors that are compared. For example, even though two vectors seem relatively similar, the scale of the features can affect the value of the Euclidean distance. In this case, the Cosine distance measure is more appropriate, as it is less susceptible to scale. The cosine angle between the two vectors would have been small.

K-means clustering works as follows:

1. Randomly choose k items from the data set as the initial center for k clusters.

2. For each of the remaining items, assign each one of them to the k clusters based on the distance between the item and the cluster centers.

3. Compute the new center for each of the clusters.

4. Keep repeating step 2 and 3 until there are no more changes to the clusters, or when the maximum number of iterations is reached.

To illustrate, Figure 4-6 presents a data set for k-means clustering. There are three distinct clusters in this data, which are illustrated with different colors.

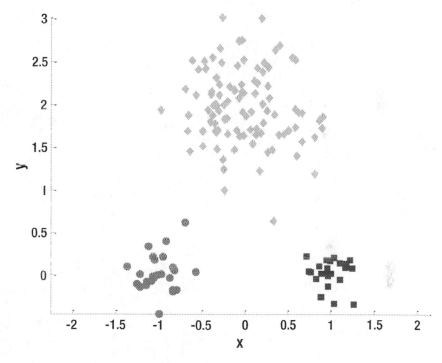

Figure 4-6. *Data set for k-means clustering*

Figure 4-7 illustrates k-means clustering with k=3 and how the three cluster centroids, represented as + symbols, move each iteration to reduce the mean squared error and more accurately reflect the cluster centers.

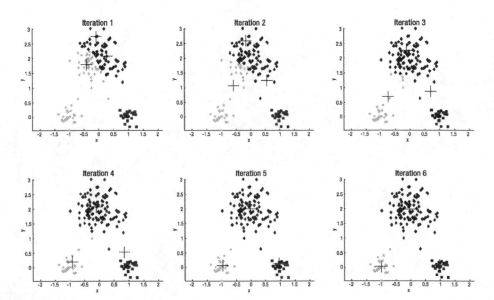

Figure 4-7. *Iterations of the K-means clustering algorithm with k=3 in which the cluster centroids are moving to minimize error*

The **K-Means Clustering** module in Azure Machine Learning supports different centroid initialization algorithms. This is specified by the **Initialization** property. Five centroid initialization algorithms are supported. Table 4-1 shows the different centroid initialization methods supported.

Table 4-1. *K-Means Cluster - Centroid Initialization Algorithms*

Centroid Initialization Algorithm	Description
Default	Picks first N points as initial centroids
Random	Picks initial centroids randomly
K-Means++	K-Means++ centroid initialization
K-Means+ Fast	K-Means++ centroid initialization with P:=1 (where the farthest centroid is picked in each iteration of the algorithm)
Evenly	Picks N points evenly as initial centroids

Summary

In this chapter, you learned about different regression, classification, and clustering algorithms. You learned how each of the algorithms work, and the type of problems for which they are suited. The goal of this chapter is to provide you with the foundation for using these algorithms to solve the various problems covered in the upcoming book chapters. In addition, the resources provided in this chapter will help you learn more deeply about the state-of-art in machine learning, and the theory behind some of these algorithms.

PART 3

Practical Applications

■ ■ ■

## CHAPTER 5

Building Customer Propensity Models

This chapter will provide a practical guide for building machine learning models. It focuses on buyer propensity models, showing how to apply the data science process to this business problem. Through a step-by-step guide, this chapter will explain how to apply key concepts and leverage the capabilities of Microsoft Azure Machine Learning for propensity modeling.

The Business Problem

Imagine that you are a marketing manager of a large bike manufacturer. You have to run a mailing campaign to entice more customers to buy your bikes. You have a limited budget and your management wants you to maximize the return on investment (ROI). So the goal of your mailing campaign is to find the best prospective customers who will buy your bikes.

With an unlimited budget the task is easy: you can simply buy lists and mail everyone. However, this brute force approach is wasteful and will yield a limited ROI since it will simply amount to junk mail for most recipients. It is very unlikely that you will meet your goals with this untargeted approach since it will lead to very low response rates.

A better approach is to use predictive analytics to target the best potential customers for your bikes, such as customers who are most likely to buy bikes. This class of predictive analytics is called buyer propensity models or customer targeting models. With this approach, you build models that predict the likelihood that a prospective customer will respond to your mailing campaign.

In this chapter, we will show you how to build this class of models in Azure Machine Learning. With the finished model you will score prospective customers and only mail those who are most likely to respond to your campaign. We will also show how you can maximize the ROI on your limited marketing budget.

■ **Note**   You will need to have an account on Azure Machine Learning. Refer to Chapter 2 for instructions to set up your new account if you do not have one yet.

As you saw in Chapter 1, the data science process typically follows these five steps.

1. Define the business problem.

2. Data acquisition and preparation.

3. Model development.

4. Model deployment.

5. Monitor model performance.

Having defined the business problem, you will explore data acquisition and preparation, model development, and evaluation in the rest of this chapter.

Data Acquisition and Preparation

In this section, you will see how to load data from different sources and analyze it in Azure Machine Learning. Azure Machine Learning enables you to load data from several sources including your local machine, the Web, a SQL database on Azure, Hive tables, or Azure Blob Storage.

Loading Data from Your Local File System

The easiest way to load data is from your local machine. Follow these steps.

1. Point your browser to the URL `https://studio.azureml.net` and log into your workspace in Azure Machine Learning.

2. Next, click the **Experiments** item from the menu on the left pane.

3. Click the **+New** button at the bottom left side of the window, and then select **Dataset** from the new menu shown in Figure 5-1.

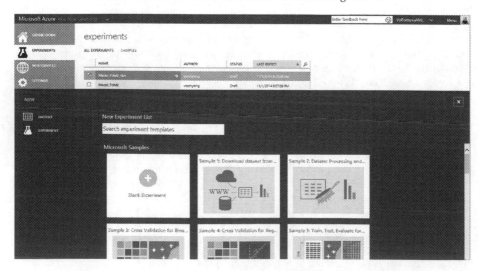

Figure 5-1. *Loading a new dataset from your local machine*

4. When you choose the option **From Local File** you will be prompted to select the data file to load from your machine.

You used these steps to load the BikeBuyer.csv file from your local file system into Azure Machine Learning.

Loading Data from Other Sources

You can load data from non-local sources using the Reader module in Azure Machine Learning. Specifically, with the Reader module you can load data from the Web, a SQL database on Azure, Azure table, Azure Blob storage, or Hive tables. To do this you will have to create a new experiment before calling the Reader module. Use the following steps to load data from any of the above sources with the Reader module.

1. Point your browser to the URL https://studio.azureml.net and log into your workspace in Azure Machine Learning.

2. Next, click the **Experiments** item from the menu on the left pane.

3. Click the +**New** button at the bottom left side of the window, and then select **Experiment** from the new menu. A new experiment is launched with a blank canvas, as shown in Figure 5-2.

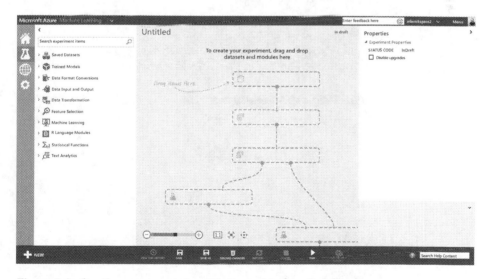

Figure 5-2. *Starting a new experiment in Azure Machine Learning*

4. Open the **Data Input and Output** menu item and you will see two modules, **Reader** and **Writer**.

5. Drag the **Reader** module from the menu to any position on the canvas.

6. Click the **Reader** module in the canvas and its properties will be shown on the right pane under **Reader**. Now specify the data source in the dropdown menu and then enter the values of all required parameters. Figure 5-3 shows the completed parameters we entered to read the BikeBuyer.csv file from our Azure Blob storage account. The Account Name and Account Key refer to a storage account on Microsoft Azure. You can obtain these parameters from the Azure portal as follows.

   a. Login to Microsoft Azure at http://azure.microsoft.com.

   b. On the top menu, click **Portal**. This takes you to the Azure portal.

   c. Select **storage** from the menu on the left pane. This lists all your storage accounts in the right pane.

   d. Click the storage account that contains the data you need for your machine learning model.

   e. At the bottom of the screen, click the key icon labeled **Manage Access Keys**. Your storage account name and access keys will be displayed. Use the Primary Access Key as your Account Key in the **Reader** module in Azure Machine Learning.

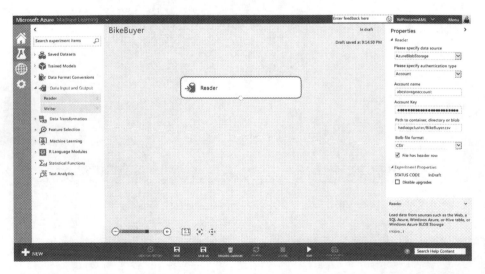

Figure 5-3. *Loading the BikeBuyer.csv file from Azure Blob storage using the Reader module*

■ **Note** You can load several datasets from multiple sources into Azure Machine Learning using the above instructions. Note, however, that each Reader module only loads a single dataset at a time.

Data Analysis

With the data loaded in Azure Machine Learning, the next step is to do pre-processing to prepare the data for modeling. It is always very useful to visualize the data as part of this process. You can visualize the Bike Buyer dataset either from the Reader module or by selecting BikeBuyer.csv from the Saved Datasets menu item in the left pane. When you hover over the small circle at the bottom of the Reader module, a menu is opened giving you two options: **Download** or **Visualize**. See Figure 5-4 for details. If you choose the Download option, you can save the data to your local machine and open it in Excel to view the data. Alternatively, you can visualize the data in Azure Machine Learning by choosing the Visualize option.

Figure 5-4. *Two options for visualizing data in Azure Machine Learning*

If you choose the Visualize option, the data will be rendered in a new window, as shown in Figure 5-5. Figure 5-5 shows the BikeBuyer.csv dataset that has historical sales data on all customers. You can see that this dataset has 10,000 rows and 13 columns including demographic variables such as marital status, gender, yearly income, number of children, occupation, age, etc. Other variables include home ownership status, number of cars, and commute distance. The last column, called Bike Buyer, is very important since it shows which customers bought bikes from your stores in the past.

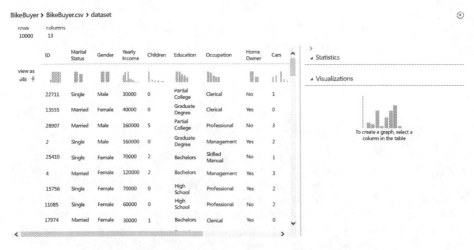

Figure 5-5. *Visualizing the Bike Buyer dataset in Azure Machine Learning*

Figure 5-5 also shows descriptive statistics such as mean, median, standard deviation, etc. for all variables in the dataset. In addition, it shows the data type of each variable and the number of missing values. By scrolling down you will see a sample of the dataset showing actual values.

The first row at the top of the feature list is a set of thumbnails showing the distribution of each variable. You can see the full distribution by clicking on the thumbnail. For instance, if you click the thumbnail above yearly income, Azure Machine Learning opens the full histogram in the right pane of the screen; this is shown in Figure 5-6. This histogram shows you the distribution of the selected variable, and you can start to think about the ways in which it can be used in your model. For instance, in Figure 5-6, you can see clearly that yearly income is not drawn from a normal distribution. If anything, it looks more like a lognormal distribution. You can also spot outliers in the histogram. Azure Machine Learning lets you overlay a probability density function or a cumulative distribution on the histogram.

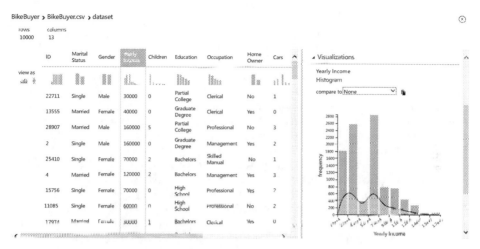

Figure 5-6. *A histogram of yearly income*

With Azure Machine Learning, you can also transform your data to a log scale. This is an important technique for capturing valid outliers that cannot be dropped. For instance, if your prospective targets include high income customers, it would be unwise to simply drop high income people as outliers. Log transformation is a better way to capture extreme incomes. Figure 5-7 shows the yearly income transformed with the log scale on the x-axis.

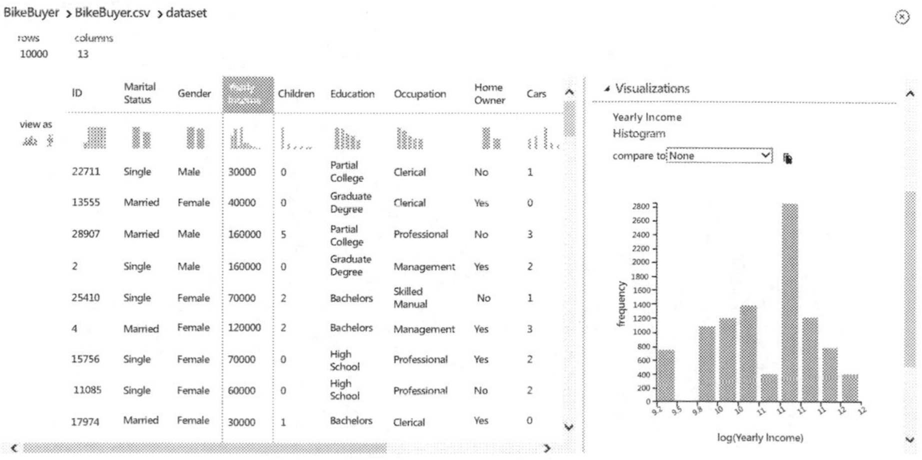

Figure 5-7. *Transforming yearly income on a log scale*

Another useful visualization tool in Azure Machine Learning is the box-and-whisker plot that is widely used in statistics. You can visualize your continuous variables with a box-and-whisker plot instead of a histogram. To do this, select the box-and-whisker icon in the first thumbnail labeled **view as**.

Figure 5-8 shows yearly income as a box-and-whisker plot instead of a histogram. On this plot, the y-value at the bottom of the box is the 25th percentile and the value at the top of the box is the 75th percentile. The line in the middle of the box is the median yearly income. The box-and-whisker plot shows outliers much more clearly: in Figure 5-8 the outliers are shown as three dots above the edge of the whisker. How are outliers determined? A rule of thumb is that any point that lies above or below 1.5*IQR is an outlier. IQR is the interquartile range measured as the 75th percentile - 25th percentile. On the box-and-whisker plot, IQR is the distance between the top and bottom of the box. Since you don't plan to drop the outliers in this case, a good alternative is to transform yearly income with the log function. The result is shown in Figure 5-9. Now you see that after the log transformation the three dots disappear from the box-and-whisker plot. This means the three extreme yearly incomes no longer appear as outliers. This is a great way to include valid extreme values in your model. This treatment can also increase the power of your predictive model.

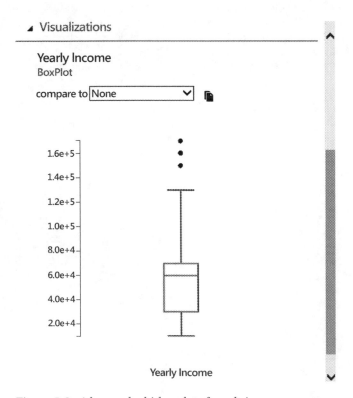

Figure 5-8. *A box-and-whisker plot of yearly income*

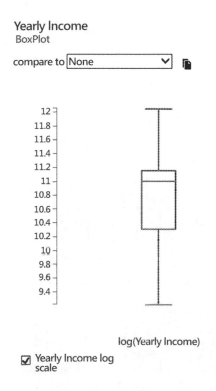

Yearly Income
BoxPlot

compare to None ▼

log(Yearly Income)

☑ Yearly Income log scale

Figure 5-9. A box-and-whisker plot of the log of yearly income

More Data Treatment

In addition to visualization, Azure Machine Learning provides many other options for data pre-processing. The menu on the left pane has many modules organized by function. Many of these modules are useful for data pre-processing.

The **Data Format Conversions** item has five different modules for converting data formats. For instance, the module named **Convert to CSV** converts data from different types such as **Dataset, DataTableDotNet**, etc., to CSV format.

The **Data Transformation** item in the menu has sub-categories for data filtering, data manipulation, data sampling, and scaling. The menu item named **Statistical Functions** also has many relevant modules for data pre-processing.

Figure 5-10 shows some of these modules in action. The **Join** module (found under the **Manipulation** sub-category) enables you to join datasets. For instance, if there was a second relevant data for the propensity model, you could use the Join module to join it with the Bike Buyer dataset.

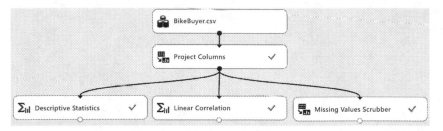

Figure 5-10. *More options for data preparation*

The module named **Descriptive Statistics** shows descriptive statistics of your dataset. For example, if you click the small circle at the bottom of this module, Azure Machine Learning shows descriptive statistics such as mean, median, standard deviation, skewness kurtosis, etc. of the Bike Buyer dataset. It also shows the number of missing values in each variable. As a rule of thumb, if a variable has 40% or more missing values, it can be dropped from the analysis, unless it is business critical.

You can resolve missing values with the module named **Missing Values Scrubber**. Like any other module in Azure Machine Learning, when you select this module, its parameters are shown on the right pane. This module allows you to handle missing values in a number of ways. First, you can remove columns with missing values. By default, the tool keeps all variables with missing values. Second, you can replace missing values with a hard-coded value in the parameter box. By default, the tool will replace any missing values with the number 0. Alternatively, you can replace missing values with the mean, median, or mode of the given variable.

The **Linear Correlation** module is also useful for computing the correlation of variables in your dataset. If you click on the small circle at the bottom of the Linear Correlation module, and then select Visualize, the tool displays a correlation matrix. In this matrix, you can see the pairwise correlation of all variables in the dataset. This module calculates the Pearson correlation coefficient. So other correlation types such as Spearman are not supported by this module. In addition, note that this module only calculates the correlation for continuous variables. For categorical variables, the module shows NaN.

Feature Selection

Feature selection is a very important part of data pre-processing. Also known as variable selection, this is the process of finding the right variables to use in the predictive model. It is particularly critical when dealing with large datasets involving hundreds of variables. Throwing over 600 variables at a predictive model is wasteful of computer resources, and also reduces its predictive accuracy. Through feature selection you can find the most influential variables for the prediction. Since the Bike Buyer dataset only has 13 variables, you could skip this step. However, let's see how to do feature selection in Azure Machine Learning because it is very important for large datasets.

To do feature selection in Azure Machine Learning, drag the module named **Filter Based Feature Selection** from the list of modules in the left pane. You can find this module by searching for it in the search box or by opening the **Feature Selection** category. To use this module, you need to connect it to a dataset as the input. Figure 5-11 shows it in use as a feature selection for the Bike Buyer dataset. Before running the experiment, use the **Launch column selector** in the right pane to define the target variable for prediction. In this case, choose the column **Bike Buyer** as the target since this is what you have to predict.

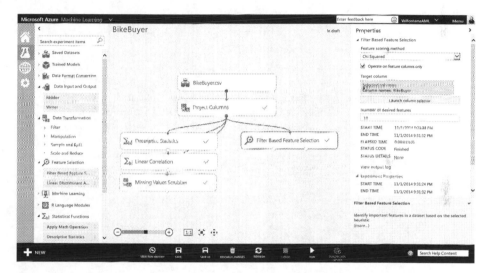

Figure 5-11. *Feature selection in Azure Machine Learning*

You also need to choose the scoring method that will be used for feature selection. Azure Machine Learning offers the following options for scoring:

- Pearson correlation

- Mutual information

- Kendall correlation

- Spearman correlation

- Chi Squared

- Fischer score

- Count based

The correlation methods find the set of variables that are highly correlated with the output, but have low correlation among themselves. The correlation is calculated using Pearson, Kendall, or Spearman correlation coefficients, depending on the option you choose.

The Fisher score uses the Fisher criterion from Statistics to rank variables. In contrast, the mutual information option is an information theoretic approach that uses mutual information to rank variables. The mutual information measures the dependence between the probability density of each variable and that of the outcome variable.

Finally, the Chi Squared option selects the best features using a test for independence; in other words, it tests whether each variable is independent of the outcome variable. It then ranks the variables based on the Chi Squared test.

▓ **Note**   See http://en.wikipedia.org/wiki/Feature_selection#Correlation _feature_selection or http://jmlr.org/papers/volume3/guyon03a/guyon03a.pdf for more information on feature selection strategies.

When you run the experiment, the **Filter Based Feature Selection** module produces two outputs. First, the filtered dataset lists the actual data for the most important variables. Second, the module shows a list of the variables by importance with the scores for each selected variable. Figure 5-12 shows the results of the features. In this case, you set the number of features to five and you used Chi Squared for scoring. Figure 5-12 shows six columns since the results set includes the target variable (i.e. Bike Buyer) plus the top ten variables, including age, cars, commute distance, education, and region. The last row of the results shows the score for each selected variable. Since the variables are ranked, the scores decrease from left to right.

Figure 5-12. *The results of feature selection for the Bike Buyer dataset with the top variables*

Note that the selected variables will vary based on the scoring method. So it is worth experimenting with different scoring methods before choosing the final set of variables. The Chi Squared and Mutual Information scoring methods produced a similar ranking of variables for the BikeBuyer dataset.

Training the Model

Once the data pre-processing is done, you are ready to train the predictive model. The first step is to choose the right type of algorithm for the problem at hand. For a propensity model, you will need a classification algorithm since your target variable is Boolean. The goal of your model is to predict whether a prospective customer will buy your bikes or not. Hence, it is a great example of a binary classification problem. As you saw in Chapters 1 and 4, classification algorithms use supervised learning for training. The training data has known outcomes for each feature set; in other words, each row in the historical data has the Bike Buyer field that shows whether the customer bought a bike or not. The Bike Buyer field is the dependent variable (also known as the response variable) that you have to predict. The input variables are the predictors (also known as independent variables or regressors) such as age, cars, commuting distance, education, region, etc. If you use logistic regression, your model can be represented as follows:

$$BikeBuyer = \frac{1}{1 + e^{(\beta_0 + \beta_1 Age + \beta_2 Cars + \beta_3 Commute\_dis\tan ce + \cdots + \varepsilon)}}$$

where β_0 is a constant which is the intercept of the regression line; β_1, β_2, β_3, etc. are the coefficients of the independent variables. ε is the error that represents the variability in the data that is not explained by the selected variables. In this equation, $BikeBuyer$ is the probability that a customer will buy a bike. Its value ranges from 0 to 1. Age, $cars$, and $Commute\_distance$ are the predictor variables.

During training, you present both the input and the output variables to the selected algorithm. At each learning iteration, the algorithm will try to predict the known outcome, using the current weights that have been learned so far. Initially, the prediction error is high because the weights have not been learned adequately. In subsequent iterations, the algorithm will adjust its weights to reduce the predictive error to the minimum. Note that each algorithm uses a different strategy to adjust the weights such that predictive error can be reduced. See Chapter 4 for more details on the statistical and machine learning algorithms in Azure Machine Learning.

Azure Machine Learning offers a wide range of classification algorithms from multiclass decision forest and jungle to two-class logistic regression, neural network, and support vector machines. For a customer propensity model, a two-class classification algorithm is appropriate since the response variable (Bike Buyer) has two classes. So you can use any of the two-class algorithms under the **Classification** sub-category. To see the full list of algorithms, expand the category named **Initialize Model** in the left pane. Expand the sub-category named **Classification** and Azure Machine Learning will list all available classification algorithms. We recommend experimenting with a few of these algorithms until you find the best one for the job. Figure 5-13 shows a simple but complete experiment for the bike buyer propensity model.

BikeBuyerModel

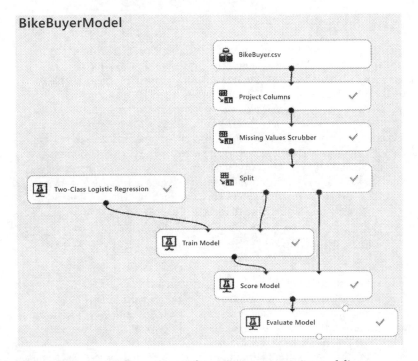

Figure 5-13. *A simple experiment for customer propensity modeling*

The **Project Columns** module simply excluded the column named ID since it is not relevant to the model. Use the **Missing Values Scrubber** module to handle missing values as discussed in the previous section. The **Split** module splits the data into two samples, one for training and the second for testing. In this experiment, you reserved 70% of the data for training and the remaining 30% for testing. This is one strategy commonly used to avoid over-fitting. Without the test sample, the model can easily memorize the data and noise. In that case, it will show very high accuracy for the training data but will perform poorly when tested with unseen data in production. Another good strategy to avoid over-fitting is cross-validation; this will be discussed later in this chapter.

Two modules are used for training the predictive model: the **Two-class Logistic Regression** module implements the logistic regression algorithm, while the **Train Model** actually does the training. The **Train Model** module trains any suitable algorithm to which it is connected. So it can be used to train any of the classification modules discussed earlier, such as **Two-class Boosted Decision Tree, Two-class Decision Forest, Two-class Decision Jungle, Two-class Neural Network,** or **Two-class Support Vector Machine**.

Model Testing and Validation

After the model is trained, the next step is to test it with a hold-out sample to avoid over-fitting. In this example, your test set is the 30% sample you created earlier with the Split module. Figure 5-13 shows how you use the module named **Score Model** to test the trained model.

Finally, the module named **Evaluate Model** is used to evaluate the performance of the model. Figure 5-13 shows how to use this module to evaluate the model's performance on the test sample. The next section also provides more details on model evaluation.

As mentioned earlier, another strategy for avoiding over-fitting is cross-validation where you use not just two, but multiple samples of the data to train and test the model. Azure Machine Learning uses 10-fold validation where the original dataset is split into 10 samples. Figure 5-14 shows a modified experiment that uses cross-validation as well as the train and test set approach. On the right track of the experiment you replace the two modules, **Train Model** and **Score Model**, with the **Cross Validate Model** module. You can check the results of the cross-validation by clicking the **small circle** on the bottom right hand side of the Cross Validate Model module. This shows the performance of each of the 10 models.

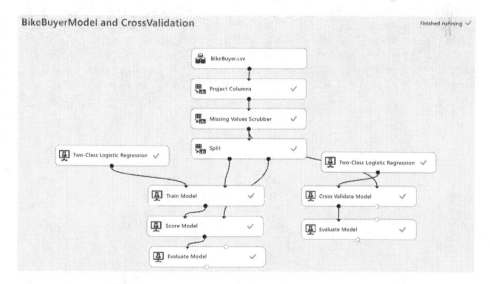

Figure 5-14. *A modified experiment with cross-validation*

Model Performance

The **Evaluate Model** module is used to measure the performance of a trained model. This module takes two datasets as inputs. The first is a scored dataset from a tested model. The second is an optional dataset for comparison. After running the experiment you can check your model's performance by clicking the **small circle** at the bottom of the module **Evaluate Model**. This module provides the following metrics to measure the performance of a classification model such as the propensity model:

- The **Receiver Operating Characteristic** (ROC) curve that plots the rate of true positives to false positives.

- The **Lift curve** (also known as the Gains curve) that plots the number of true positives versus the positive rate. This is popular in marketing.

- **Precision versus recall** chart.

- **Confusion matrix** that shows type I and II errors.

Figure 5-15 shows the ROC curve for the propensity model you built earlier. The ROC curve visually shows the performance of a predictive binary classification model. The diagonal line from (0,0) to (1,1) on the chart shows the performance of random guessing; so if you randomly selected who to target, your response would be on this diagonal line. A good predictive model should do much better than random guesses. Hence, on the ROC curve, a good model should fall above the diagonal line. The ideal model that is 100% accurate will have a vertical line from (0,0) to (0,1), followed by a horizontal line from (0,1) to (1,1).

BikeBuyerModel and CrossValidation ❯ Evaluate Model ❯ Evaluation results

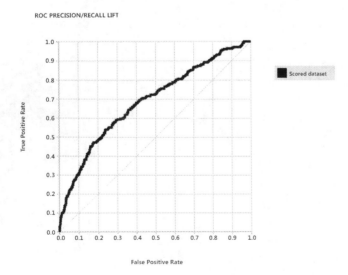

Figure 5-15. The ROC curve for the customer propensity model

One way to measure the performance from the ROC curve is to measure the area under the curve (AUC). The higher the area under the curve, the better the model's performance. The ideal model will have an AUC of 1.0, while a random guess will have an AUC of 0.5. The logistic regression model you built has an AUC of 0.689, which is much better random guess!

Figure 5-16 shows the confusion matrix for the logistic regression model you built earlier. The confusion matrix has four cells, namely

- **True positives**: These are cases where the customer actually bought a bike and the model correctly predicts this.

- **True negatives**: In the historical dataset these customers did not buy bikes, and the model correctly predicts that they would not buy.

- **False positives**: In this case, the model incorrectly predicts that the customer would buy a bike when in fact they did not. This is commonly referred to as Type I error. The logistic regression you built had only two false positives.

- **False negatives**: Here the model incorrectly predicts that the customer would not buy a bike when in real life the customer did buy one. This is also known as Type II error. The logistic regression model had up to 276 false negatives.

True Positive	False Negative	Accuracy	Precision	Threshold	AUC
3	276	0.907	0.600	0.5	0.689

False Positive	True Negative	Recall	F1 Score
2	2719	0.011	0.021

Score bin	# Pos	# Neg	Pop.above thresh.	Accuracy	F1	+ve Prec.	+ve Rec.(= TPR)	-ve Prec.	-ve Rec.(= 1 - FPR)	Cumulative AUC
(0.900,1.000]	0	0	0.000	0.907	0.000	1.000	0.000	0.907	1.000	0.000
(0.800,0.900]	0	0	0.000	0.907	0.000	1.000	0.000	0.907	1.000	0.000
(0.700,0.800]	0	0	0.000	0.907	0.000	1.000	0.000	0.907	1.000	0.000
(0.600,0.700]	1	0	0.000	0.907	0.007	1.000	0.004	0.907	1.000	0.000
(0.500,0.600]	0	2	0.001	0.907	0.007	0.333	0.004	0.907	0.999	0.000
(0.400,0.500]	6	2	0.004	0.908	0.048	0.636	0.025	0.909	0.999	0.000
(0.300,0.400]	13	14	0.013	0.908	0.126	0.526	0.072	0.913	0.993	0.000
(0.200,0.300]	42	133	0.071	0.877	0.252	0.291	0.222	0.922	0.945	0.008
(0.100,0.200]	122	885	0.407	0.623	0.245	0.151	0.659	0.947	0.619	0.165
(0.000,0.100]	95	1685	1.000	0.093	0.170	0.093	1.000	1.000	0.000	0.689

Figure 5-16. *Confusion matrix and more performance metrics*

In addition, Figure 5-16 also shows the accuracy, precision, and recall of the model. Here are the formulas for these metrics.

Precision is the rate of true positives in the results.

$$Precision = \frac{tp}{tp+fp} = \frac{3}{3+2} = 0.6$$

Recall is the percentage of buyers that the model identifies and is measured as

$$Recall = \frac{tp}{tp+fn} = \frac{3}{3+276} = 0.011$$

Finally, the accuracy measures how well the model correctly identifies buyers and non-buyers, as in

$$Accuracy = \frac{tp+tn}{tp+tn+fp+fn} = \frac{3+2719}{3+2719+2+276} = 0.907$$

where tp = true positive, tn = true negative, fp = false positive, and fn = false negative.

You can also compare the performance of two models on a single ROC chart. As an example, let's modify the experiment in Figure 5-14 to use the **Two-class Boosted Decision tree** module as the second trainer instead of the **Two-class Logistic Regression** module. Now your experiment has two different classifiers, the Two-class Logistic Regression on the left branch and the Two-class Boosted Decision Tree on the right branch. You connect the scored datasets from both models into the same **Evaluate Model** module. The updated experiment is shown in Figure 5-17 and the results are illustrated in Figure 5-18. On this chart, the curve labeled "scored dataset to compare" is the ROC curve for the **Two-class Boosted Decision Tree** model, while the one labeled "scored dataset" is the one for the **Two-class Logistic Regression**. You can see clearly that the boosted decision tree model outperforms the logistic regression model, as it has a higher lift over the diagonal line for random guesses. The area under the curve (AUC) for the boosted decision tree model is 0.722, which is better than that of the logistic regression model, which was 0.689, as you saw earlier.

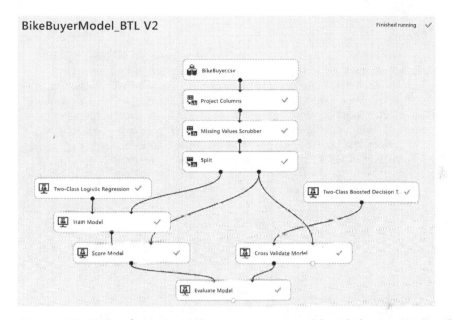

Figure 5-17. *Updated experiment that compares two models with the same Evaluate Model module*

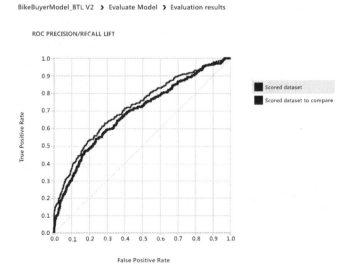

Figure 5-18. *ROC curves comparing the performance of two predictive models, the boosted decision tree versus logistic regression*

Summary

In this chapter, we provided a practical guide on how to build buyer propensity models with the Microsoft Azure Machine Learning service. Through a step-by-step guide in this chapter we explained how to build buyer propensity models in Microsoft Azure Machine Learning service. You learned how to perform data pre-processing and analysis, which are critical steps towards understanding the data that you are using for building customer propensity models. With that understanding of the data, you used a two-class logistic regression and a two-class boosted decision tree algorithm to perform classification. You also saw how to evaluate the performance of your models and avoid over-fitting.

■ ■ ■

## CHAPTER 6

Building Churn Models

In this chapter, we reveal the secrets of building customer churn models, which are in very high demand. Many industries use churn analysis as a means of reducing customer attrition. This chapter will show a holistic view of building customer churn models in Microsoft Azure Machine Learning.

Churn Models in a Nutshell

Businesses need to have an effective strategy for managing customer churn because it costs more to attract new customers than to retain existing ones. Customer churn can take different forms, such as switching to a competitor's service, reducing the time spent using the service, reducing the number of services used, or switching to a lower-cost service. Companies in the retail, media, telecommunication, and banking industries use churn modeling to create better products, services, and experiences that lead to a higher customer retention rate.

Let's drill deeper into why churn modeling matters to telecommunication companies. The consumer business of many telecommunication companies operates in an immensely competitive market. In many countries, it is common to have two or more telecommunication companies competing for the same customer. In addition, mobile number portability makes it easier for customers to switch to another telecommunication provider.

Many telecommunication companies track churn levels as part of their annual report. The use of churn models has enabled telecommunication providers to formulate effective business strategies for customer retention, and to prevent potential revenue loss.

Churn models enable companies to predict which customers are most likely to churn, and to understand the factors that cause churn to occur. Among the different machine learning techniques used to build churn models, classification algorithms are commonly used. Azure Machine Learning provides a wide range of classification algorithms including decision forest, decision jungle, logistic regression, neural networks, Bayes point machines, and support vector machines. Figure 6-1 shows the different classification algorithms that you can use in Azure Machine Learning Studio.

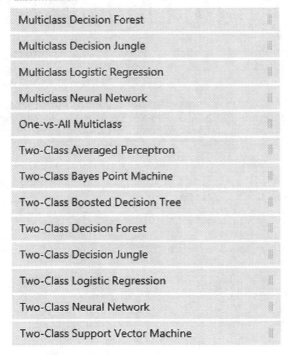

Figure 6-1. *Classification algorithms available in ML Studio*

Prior to building the churn model (based on classification algorithms), understanding the data is very important. Given a dataset that you are using for both training and testing the churn model, you should ask the following questions (non-exhaustive) about the data:

- What kind of information is captured in each column?

- Should you use the information in each column directly, or should you compute derived values from each column that are more meaningful?

- What is the data distribution?

- Are the values in each column numeric or categorical?

- Does a column consists of many missing values?

Once you understand the data, you can start building the churn model using the following steps.

1. Data preparation and understanding

2. Data preprocessing and feature selection

3. Classification model for predicting customer churn

4. Evaluating the performance of the model

5. Operationalizing the model

In this chapter, you will learn how to perform each of these steps to build a churn model for a telecommunication use case. You will learn the different tools that are available in Azure Machine Learning Studio for understanding the data and performing data preprocessing. And you will learn the different performance metrics that are used for evaluating the effectiveness of the model. Let's get started!

Building and Deploying a Customer Churn Model

In this section, you will learn how to build a customer churn model using different classification algorithms. For building the customer churn model, you will be using a telecommunication dataset from KDD Cup 2009. The dataset is provided by a leading French telecommunication company, Orange. Based on the Orange 2013 Annual Report, Orange has 236 million customers globally (15.5 million fixed broadband customers and 178.5 million mobile customers).

The goal of the KDD Cup 2009 challenge is to build an effective machine learning model for predicting customer churn, willingness to buy new products/services (appetency), and opportunities for up-selling. In this section, you will focus on predicting customer churn.

■ **Note**   KDD Cup is an annual competition organized by the ACM Special Interest Group on Knowledge Discovery and Data Mining (SIGKDD). Each year, data scientists participate in various data mining and knowledge discovery challenges. These challenges range from predicting who is most likely to donate to a charity (1997), clickstream analysis for an online retailer (2000), predicting movie rating behavior (2007), to predicting the propensity of customers to switch providers (2009).

Preparing and Understanding Data

In this exercise, you will use the small Orange dataset, which consists of 50,000 rows. Each row has 230 columns (referred to as variables). The first 190 variables are numerical and the last 40 variables are categorical.

Before you start building the experiment, download the following small dataset and the churn labels from the KDD Cup web site:

- orange_small_train.data.zip - www.sigkdd.org/site/2009/ files/orange_small_train.data.zip

- orange_small_train_churn.labels - www.sigkdd.org/ site/2009/files/orange_small_train_churn.labels

In the orange_small_train_churn.labels file, each line consists of a +1 or -1 value. The +1 value refers to a positive example (the customer churned), and the -1 value refers to a negative example (the customer did not churn).

Once the file has been uploaded, you should upload the dataset and the labels to Machine Learning Studio, as follows:

1. Click **New** and choose **Dataset ➤ From Local File** (Figure 6-2).

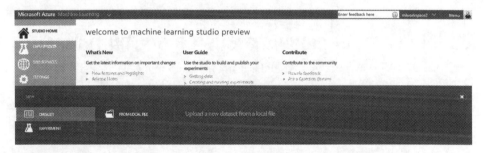

Figure 6-2. *Uploading the Orange dataset using Machine Learning Studio*

2. Next, choose the file to upload: **orange_small_train.data** (Figure 6-3) .

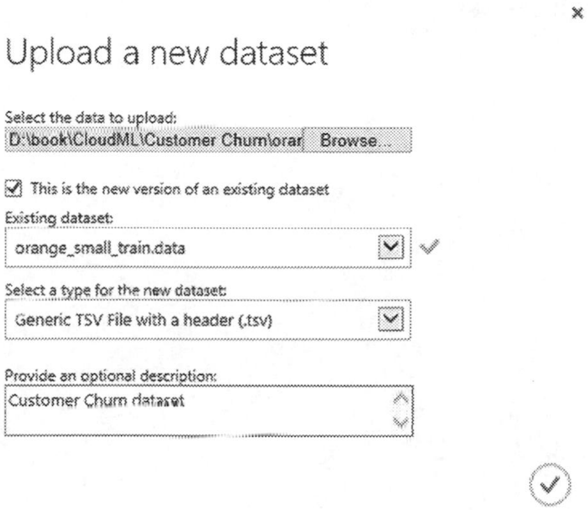

Upload a new dataset

Select the data to upload:

| D:\book\CloudML\Customer Churn\orar | Browse... |

☑ This is the new version of an existing dataset

Existing dataset:

| orange_small_train.data | ▾ | ✓ |

Select a type for the new dataset:

| Generic TSV File with a header (.tsv) | ▾ |

Provide an optional description:

| Customer Churn dataset | ↕ |

(✓)

Figure 6-3. Uploading the dataset

3. Click **OK**.

After the Orange dataset has been uploaded, repeat the steps to upload the churn labels file to Machine Learning Studio. Once this is done, you should be able to see the two Orange datasets when you create a new experiment. To do this, create a new experiment, and expand the Saved Datasets menu in the left pane. Figure 6-4 shows the Orange training and churn labels datasets that you uploaded.

Figure 6-4. *Saved Datasets, Orange Training Data and Churn Labels*

When building any machine learning model, it is very important to understand the data before trying to build the model. To do this, create a new experiment as follows.

1. Click **New ➤ Experiment**.

2. Name the experiment - **Understanding the Orange Dataset**.

3. From **Saved Datasets**, choose the **orange_small_train.data** dataset (double-click it).

4. From **Statistical Functions**, choose **Descriptive Statistics** (double-click it).

5. You will see both modules. Connect the dataset with the **Descriptive Statistics** module. Figure 6-5 shows the completed experiment.

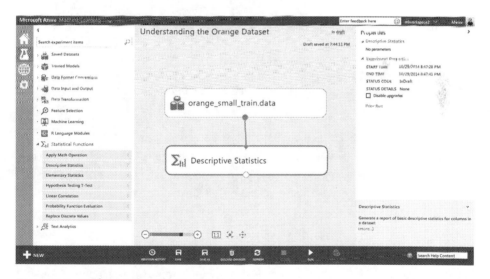

Figure 6-5. *Understanding the Orange dataset*

6. Click **Run**.

7. Once the run completes successfully, right-click the circle below **Descriptive Statistics** and choose **Visualize**.

8. You will see an analysis of the data, which covers Unique Value Count, Missing Value Count, Min, and Max for each of the variables (Figure 6-6).

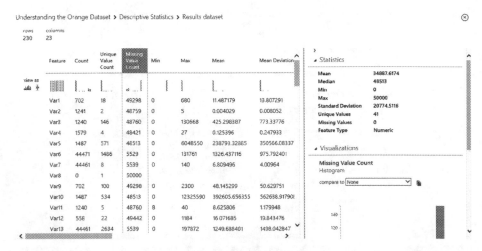

Figure 6-6. *Descriptive statistics for the Orange dataset*

This provides useful information on each of the variables. From the visualization, you will observe that there are lots of variables with missing values (e.g., Var1, Var8). For example, Var8 is practically a column with no useful information.

▓ **Tip** When visualizing the output of **Descriptive Statistics**, it shows the top 100 variables. To see all the statistics for all the 230 variables, right-click the bottom circle of **Descriptive Statistic** module and choose **Save as dataset**. After the dataset has been saved, you can choose to download the file and see all the rows in Excel.

Data Preprocessing and Feature Selection

In most classification tasks, you will often have to identify which of the variables should be used to build the model. Machine Learning Studio provides two feature selection modules that can be used to determine the right variables for modeling. This includes filter-based feature selection and linear discriminant analysis.

For this exercise, you will not be using these feature selection modules. Figure 6-7 shows the data preprocessing steps.

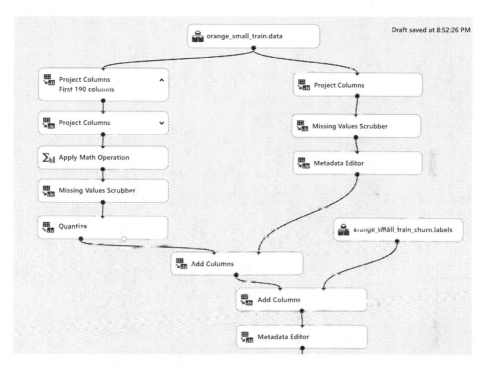

Figure 6-7. Data preprocessing steps

For simplicity, perform the following steps to preprocess the data.

1. Divide the variables into the first 190 columns (numerical data) and the remaining 40 columns (categorical data). To do this, add two **Project Columns** modules.

    For the first **Project Column** module, select **Column indices: 1-190** (Figure 6-8).

Properties   **>**

▲ Project Columns

Select columns

Selected columns:
Column indices: 1-190

                    Launch column selector

Figure 6-8. Selecting column indices 1-190 (numerical columns)

For the second **Project Column** module, select **Column indices: 191-230** (Figure 6-9).

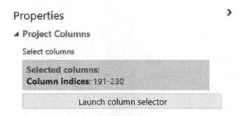

Figure 6-9. Selecting column indices 191-230 (categorical columns)

2. For the first 190 columns, do the following:

    a. Use **Project Columns** to select the columns that contain numerical data (and remove columns that contain zero or very few values). These includes the following columns: Var6, Var8, Var15, Var20, Var31, Var32, Var39, Var42, Var48, Var52, Var55, Var79, Var141, Var167, Var175, and Var185. Figure 6-10 shows the columns that are excluded.

Select columns

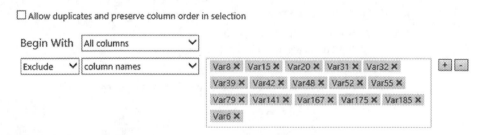

Figure 6-10. Excluding columns that do not contain useful values

    b. Apply a math operation that adds 1 to each row. The rationale is that this enables you to distinguish between rows that contain actual 0 for the column vs. the substitution value 0 (when you use the Missing Values Scrubber). Figure 6-11 shows the properties for the **Math Operation** module.

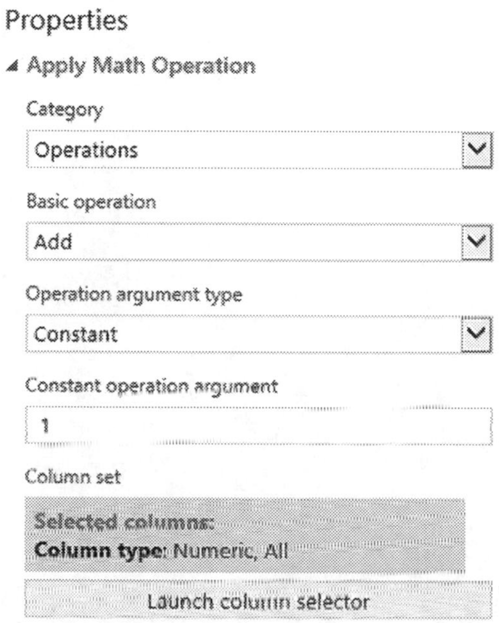

Properties

◢ Apply Math Operation

Category

| Operations | ⌄ |

Basic operation

| Add | ⌄ |

Operation argument type

| Constant | ⌄ |

Constant operation argument

| 1 |

Column set

Selected columns:
Column type: Numeric, All

Launch column selector

Figure 6-11. *Adding 1 to existing numeric variables*

      c.   Use the **Missing Value Scrubber** to substitute missing values with 0. Figure 6-12 shows the properties.

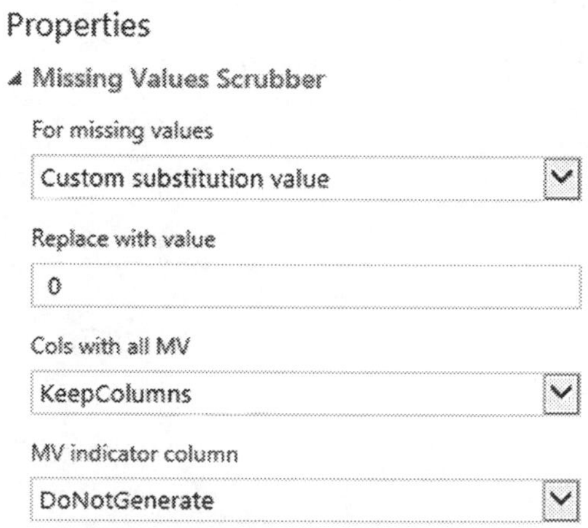

Properties

◢ Missing Values Scrubber

For missing values

| Custom substitution value | ⌄ |

Replace with value

| 0 |

Cols with all MV

| KeepColumns | ⌄ |

MV indicator column

| DoNotGenerate | ⌄ |

Figure 6-12. *Missing Values Scrubber properties*

> d.   Use the **Quantize** module to map the input values to a smaller number of bins using a quantization function. In this exercise, you will use the **EqualWidth binning** mode. Figure 6-13 shows the properties used.

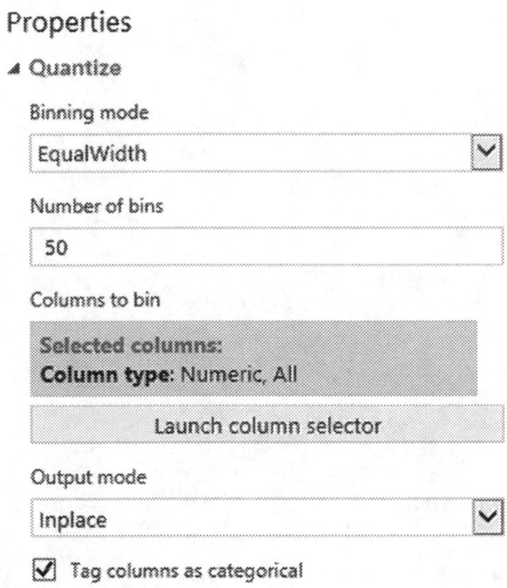

Properties

◢ Quantize

Binning mode

| EqualWidth | ∨ |

Number of bins

| 50 |

Columns to bin

Selected columns:
Column type: Numeric, All

| Launch column selector |

Output mode

| Inplace | ∨ |

☑ Tag columns as categorical

Figure 6-13. *Quantize properties*

> 3.   For the remaining 40 columns, perform the following steps:
>
> > a.   Use the **Missing Values Scrubber** to substitute it with 0. Figure 6-14 shows the properties.

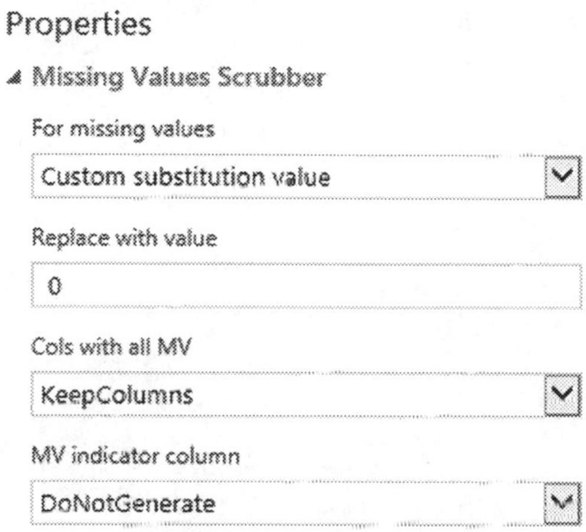

Properties

⊿ Missing Values Scrubber

For missing values

| Custom substitution value | ⌄ |

Replace with value

| 0 |

Cols with all MV

| KeepColumns | ⌄ |

MV indicator column

| DoNotGenerate | ⌄ |

Figure 6-14. *Missing Values Scrubber (for the remaining 40 columns)*

      b.   Use the **Metadata Editor** to change the type for all columns to be **categorical**. Figure 6-15 shows the properties.

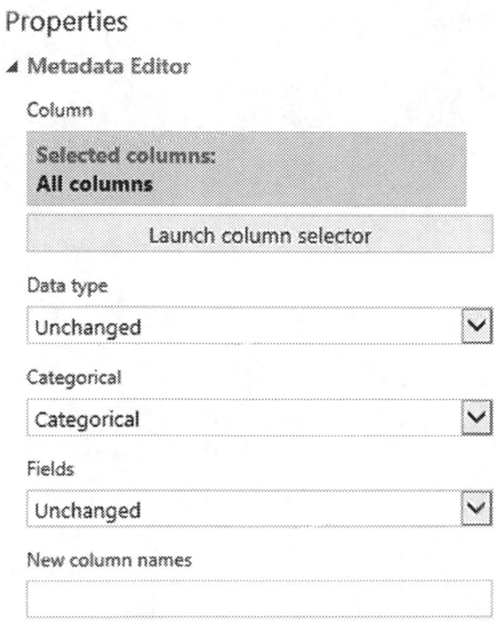

Properties

⊿ Metadata Editor

Column

Selected columns:
All columns

| Launch column selector |

Data type

| Unchanged | ⌄ |

Categorical

| Categorical | ⌄ |

Fields

| Unchanged | ⌄ |

New column names

| |

Figure 6-15. *Using the Metadata Editor to mark the columns as containing categorical data*

4.   Combine it with the labels from the **ChurnLabel** dataset.
     Figure 6-16 shows the combined data.

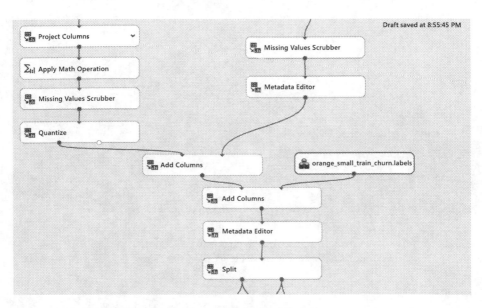

Figure 6-16. *Combining training data and training label*

5.   Rename the label column as **ChurnLabel**. Figure 6-17 shows
     how you can use the Metadata Editor to rename the column.

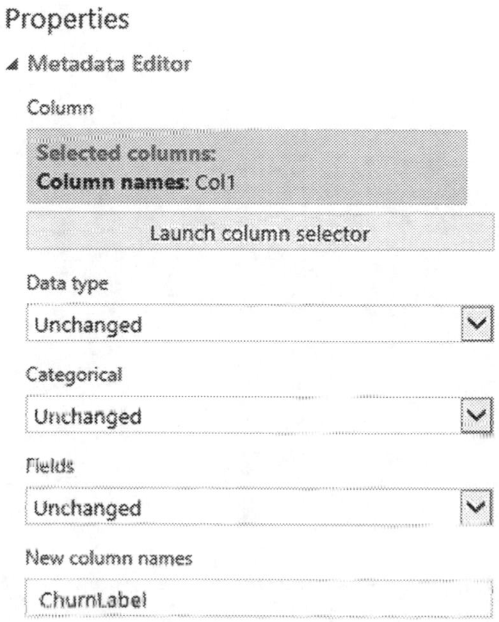

Properties

◢ Metadata Editor

Column

> Selected columns:
> **Column names:** Col1

> Launch column selector

Data type

| Unchanged | ⌄ |

Categorical

| Unchanged | ⌄ |

Fields

| Unchanged | ⌄ |

New column names

| ChurnLabel |

Figure 6-17. *Renaming the label column as ChurnLabel*

Classification Model for Predicting Churn

In this section, you will start building the customer churn model using the classification algorithms provided in Azure Machine Learning Studio. For predicting customer churn, you will use two classification algorithms, a two-class boosted decision tree and a two-class decision forest.

A decision tree is a machine learning algorithm for classification or regression. During training, it splits the data using the input variables that give the highest information gain. The process is repeated on each subset of the data until splitting is no longer required. The leaf of the decision tree identifies the label to be predicted (or class). This prediction is provided based on a probability distribution.

The boosted decision tree and decision forest algorithms build an ensemble of decision trees and use them for predictions. The key difference between the two approaches is that, in boosted decision tree algorithms, multiple decision trees are grown in series such that the output of one tree is provided as input to the next tree. This is a boosting approach to ensemble modeling. In contrast, the decision forest algorithm grows each decision tree independently of each other; each tree in the ensemble uses a sample of data drawn from the original dataset. This is the bagging approach of ensemble modeling. See Chapter 4 for more details on decision trees, decision forests, and boosted decision trees. Figure 6-18 shows how the data is split and used as inputs to train the two classification models.

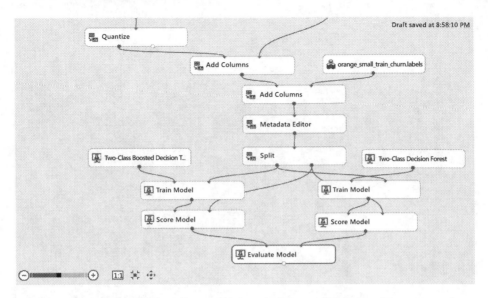

Figure 6-18. *Splitting the data into training and testing, and training the customer churn model*

From Figure 6-18, you can see that the following steps are performed.

1. Splitting the input data into training and test data: In this exercise, you split the data by specifying the **Fraction of rows in the first output** dataset, and set it as **0.7**. This assigns 70% of data to the training set and the remaining 30% to the test dataset.

    Figure 6-19 shows the properties for Split.

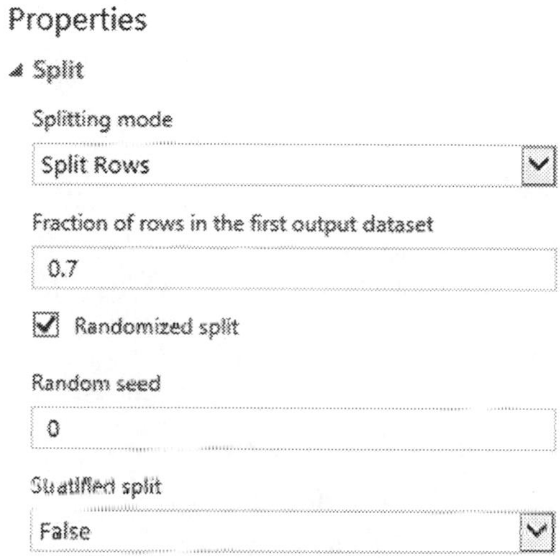

Properties

▰ Split

Splitting mode

| Split Rows | ∨ |

Fraction of rows in the first output dataset

| 0.7 |

☑ Randomized split

Random seed

| 0 |

Stratified split

| False | ∨ |

Figure 6 19. Properties of the Split module

2. Training the model using the training data: In this exercise, you will be training two classification models, a two-class boosted decision tree and two-class decision forest. Figures 6-20 and 6-21 show the properties for each of the classification algorithms.

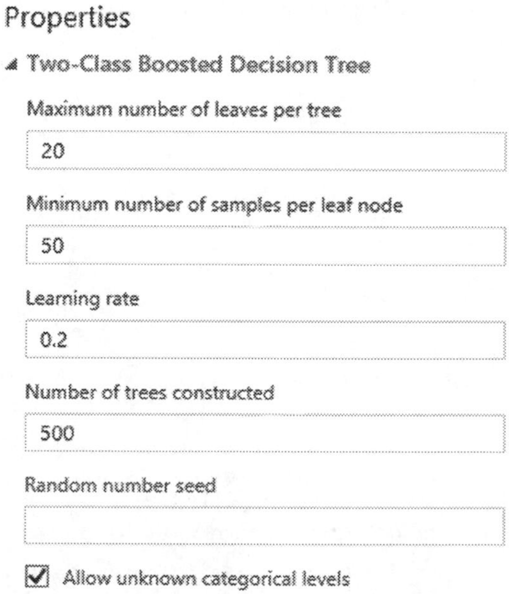

Properties

▰ Two-Class Boosted Decision Tree

Maximum number of leaves per tree

| 20 |

Minimum number of samples per leaf node

| 50 |

Learning rate

| 0.2 |

Number of trees constructed

| 500 |

Random number seed

| |

☑ Allow unknown categorical levels

Figure 6-20. Properties for two-class boosted decision tree

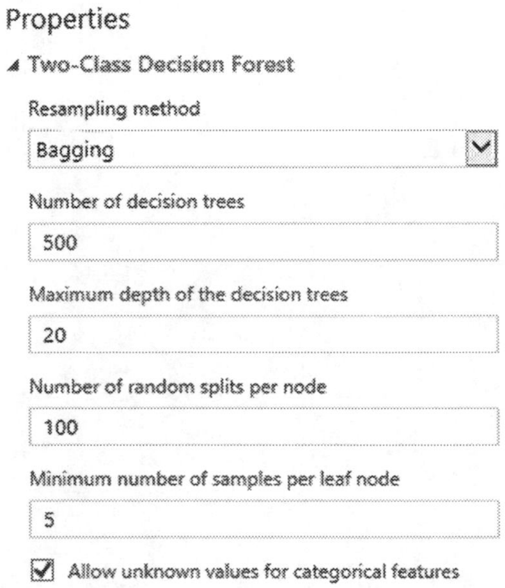

Properties

▲ Two-Class Decision Forest

Resampling method

> Bagging ⌄

Number of decision trees

> 500

Maximum depth of the decision trees

> 20

Number of random splits per node

> 100

Minimum number of samples per leaf node

> 5

☑ Allow unknown values for categorical features

Figure 6-21. *Properties for two-class decision forest*

3. Training the model using the **Train Model** module: To train the model, you need to select the label column. In this exercise, you will be using the **ChurnLabel** column. Figure 6-22 shows the properties for **Train Model**.

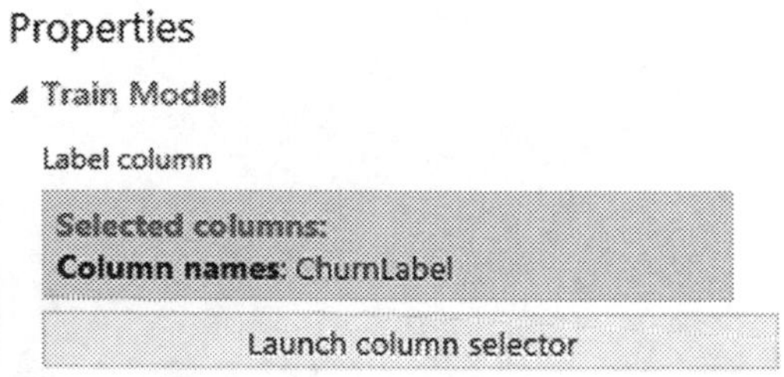

Properties

▲ Train Model

Label column

> **Selected columns:**
> **Column names**: ChurnLabel

> Launch column selector

Figure 6-22. *Using ChurnLabel as the Label column*

Scoring the model: After training the customer churn model, you can use the **Score Model** module to predict the label column for a test dataset. The output of **Score Model** will be used in **Evaluate Model** to understand the performance of the model.

Congratulations, you have successfully built a customer churn model! You learned how to use two of the classification algorithms available in Machine Learning Studio. You also learned how to evaluate the performance of the model. In the next few chapters, you will learn how to deploy the model to production and operationalize it.

Evaluating the Performance of the Customer Churn Models

After you use the **Score Model** to predict whether a customer will churn, the output of the **Score Model** module is passed to the **Evaluate Model** to generate evaluation metrics for each of the model. Figure 6-23 shows the **Score Model** and **Evaluate Model** modules.

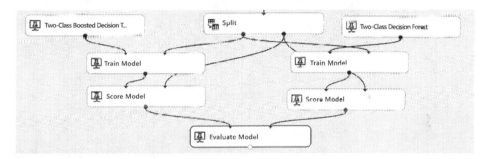

Figure 6-23. *Scoring and evaluating the model*

After you have evaluated the model, you can right-click the circle at the bottom of **Evaluate Model** to see the performance of the two customer churn models. Figure 6-24 shows the Receiver Operating Characteristic (ROC curve) while Figure 6-25 shows the accuracy, precision, recall, and F1 scores for the two customer churn models.

Customer Churn ➤ Evaluate Model ➤ Evaluation results

ROC PRECISION/RECALL LIFT

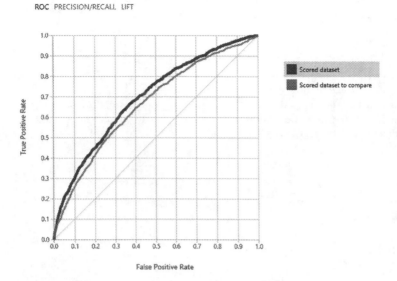

Figure 6-24. *ROC curve for the two customer churn models*

True Positive	False Negative	Accuracy	Precision	Threshold	Cumulative AUC
178	939	0.907	0.283	0.5	0.698

False Positive	True Negative	Recall	F1 Score
452	13431	0.159	0.204

Score bin	# Pos	# Neg	Pop.above thresh.	Accuracy	F1	+ve Prec.	+ve Rec.(= TPR)	-ve Prec.	-ve Rec.(= 1 - FPR)	Cumulative AUC
(0.900,1.000]	81	169	0.017	0.920	0.119	0.324	0.073	0.930	0.988	0.001
(0.800,0.900]	32	76	0.024	0.917	0.153	0.316	0.101	0.931	0.982	0.001
(0.700,0.800]	19	66	0.030	0.914	0.169	0.298	0.118	0.932	0.978	0.002
(0.600,0.700]	19	66	0.035	0.910	0.184	0.286	0.135	0.933	0.973	0.002
(0.500,0.600]	26	67	0.041	0.908	0.204	0.285	0.158	0.935	0.968	0.003
(0.400,0.500]	18	104	0.050	0.902	0.210	0.262	0.175	0.935	0.961	0.004
(0.300,0.400]	27	113	0.059	0.896	0.222	0.251	0.199	0.937	0.952	0.006
(0.200,0.300]	27	155	0.071	0.888	0.228	0.234	0.223	0.938	0.941	0.008
(0.100,0.200]	58	348	0.098	0.868	0.237	0.209	0.275	0.940	0.916	0.014
(0.000,0.100]	810	12719	1.000	0.074	0.139	0.074	1.000	1.000	0.000	0.692

Figure 6-25. *Accuracy, precision, recall, and F1 scores for the customer churn models*

The ROC curve shows the performance of the customer churn models. The diagonal line from (0,0) to (1,1) on the chart shows the performance of random guessing. For example, if you randomly guessed which customer would churn, the curve will be on the diagonal line. A good predictive model should perform better than random guessing, and the ROC curve should be above the diagonal line. The performance of a customer churn model can be measured by considering the area under the curve (AUC). The higher the area under the curve, the better the model's performance. The ideal model will have an AUC of 1.0, while a random guess will have an AUC of 0.5.

From the visualization, you can see that the customer churn models have a cumulative AUC, accuracy, and precision of 0.698, 0.907, and 0.283, respectively. You can also see that the customer models have a F1 score of 0.204.

░ **Note**   See `http://en.wikipedia.org/wiki/F1_score` for a good discussion on the use of the F1 score to measure the accuracy of the machine learning model.

Summary

Using the KDD Cup 2009 Orange telecommunication dataset, you learned step by step how to build customer churn models using Azure Machine Learning. Before building the model, you took time to first understand the data and perform data preprocessing. Next, you learned how to use the two-class boosted decision tree and two-class decision forest algorithms to perform classification, and to build a model for predicting customer churn with the telecommunication dataset. After building the model, you also learned how to measure the performance of the models.

CHAPTER 7

■ ■ ■

Customer Segmentation Models

In this chapter, you will learn how to build customer segmentation models in Microsoft Azure Machine Learning. Using a practical example, we present a step-by-step guide on using Microsoft Azure Machine Learning to easily build segmentation models using k-means clustering. After the models have been built, you will learn how to perform validation and deploy it in production.

Customer Segmentation Models in a Nutshell

In order for companies to compete effectively, and build products and services that sell, it is super important to figure out the target customer segments and the characteristics of each segment. Identifying customer segments is critical since it helps companies to better target their marketing campaigns to win the most profitable customers. Data analysts in companies are tasked with sifting through data from both internal and external data sources to identify the magical ingredients that will appeal to specific customer segments (which might not be known a priori).

Customer segmentation empowers companies with the ability to craft marketing strategies and execute marketing campaigns that target and appeal to specific customer segments. In addition, customer segmentation leads to greater customer satisfaction because different needs in different segmentations can be addressed appropriately.

■ **Note** Learn more about market segmentation at
http://en.wikipedia.org/wiki/Market_segmentation.

Companies must be able to master the deluge of information that is available (e.g. market research reports, concept/market testing, etc.). While this market research data provides a good balance of qualitative and quantitative information on the market, companies can compete even more effectively if they can tap the huge treasure trove of data that they already have (e.g. membership/loyalty program databases, billing data from online services/retail outlets, CRM systems, etc.). Somewhere in the treasure trove lies insights that companies can turn to their competitive advantage. These insights enable companies to be cognizant of potential customer segments and their characteristics.

For example, in the United States, many people arc familiar with the use of the consumer credit score. The consumer credit score helps banks understand the risk profile of customers applying for loans (auto loans, mortgage loans, etc.). This in turn enables banks to tune their interest rates based on the risk segment to which an individual belongs.

Another example is the telecommunication industry. Many telecommunication providers strive to gain insights on how to sell effectively to their customers falling into the two broad groups, corporate business and consumers. In order to figure out effective marketing strategies for consumers, telecommunication providers are often interested in the profile of the person that uses the service. Folks with similar profiles are grouped together, and offered discounts or value-added services that appeal to that profile. A non-exhaustive list of features that a telecommunication provider considers include income group, call frequency of friends and family members, number of calls/short messages and when they happened, how they pay their monthly bill (online, self-service kiosks, physical stores), delays in payment, etc.

Amongst the different types of unsupervised machine learning techniques, k-means clustering is a common technique used to perform customer segmentation. In this chapter, you will learn how to use Microsoft Azure Machine Learning to perform k-means clustering on the Wikipedia SP 500 dataset (one of the sample datasets available in ML Studio).

The Wikipedia SP 500 dataset contains the following information: industry category, and text describing each of the 500 Standard & Poor's (SP500) companies. You will build and deploy a k-means clustering model to perform segmentation of the companies. Due to the large number of features that are extracted from the text, you will execute an R script to perform principal component analysis to identify the top 10 features, which will be used for determining the clusters. After k-means clustering has been performed, companies that are similar to each other (based on features extracted from the companies' descriptive text) will be assigned to the same segment.

▓ **Note** See Chapter 4 for an overview of the different statistical and machine learning algorithms. In the chapter, you will also learn about the categories of clustering algorithms, and how K-Means Clustering works.

Building and Deploying Your First K-Means Clustering Model

To help you get started building your first k-means clustering model, you will use one of the sample experiments provided in the ML Studio. The experiment uses k-means clustering to perform segmentation of companies in the Standard & Poor's (S&P) 500 list of companies.

After the experiment is successfully executed, you can see that the companies (from different industry categories) have been assigned to different clusters (Figure 7-1). In this example, the k-means algorithm finds three segments labeled 0, 1, and 2 on the x-axis. In each of the square boxes, you will see the number of companies from each category that has been assigned to a cluster. In Cluster 2, you can see that there is 1 company from the Consumer Discretionary category.

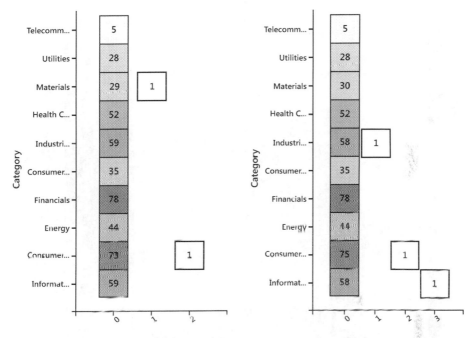

Figure 7-1. *Segmentation of the companies*

Let's get started! For this exercise, let's use the sample experiment called Sample Experiment - S & P 500 Company Clustering - Development (shown in Figure 7-2). From Figure 7-3 , you will see that the experiment consists of the following steps.

1. Retrieve the data from the Wikipedia SP 500 dataset.

2. Perform feature hashing of the data to vectorize the features.

3. Execute an R script to identify the principal components of the features.

4. Project the columns that will be used in the clustering model.

5. Train the clustering model using two k-means clustering models. For each of the k-means clustering models, different numbers of clusters are specified.

6. Convert the results to a CSV file.

In this section, you will learn how to perform segmentation of the companies.

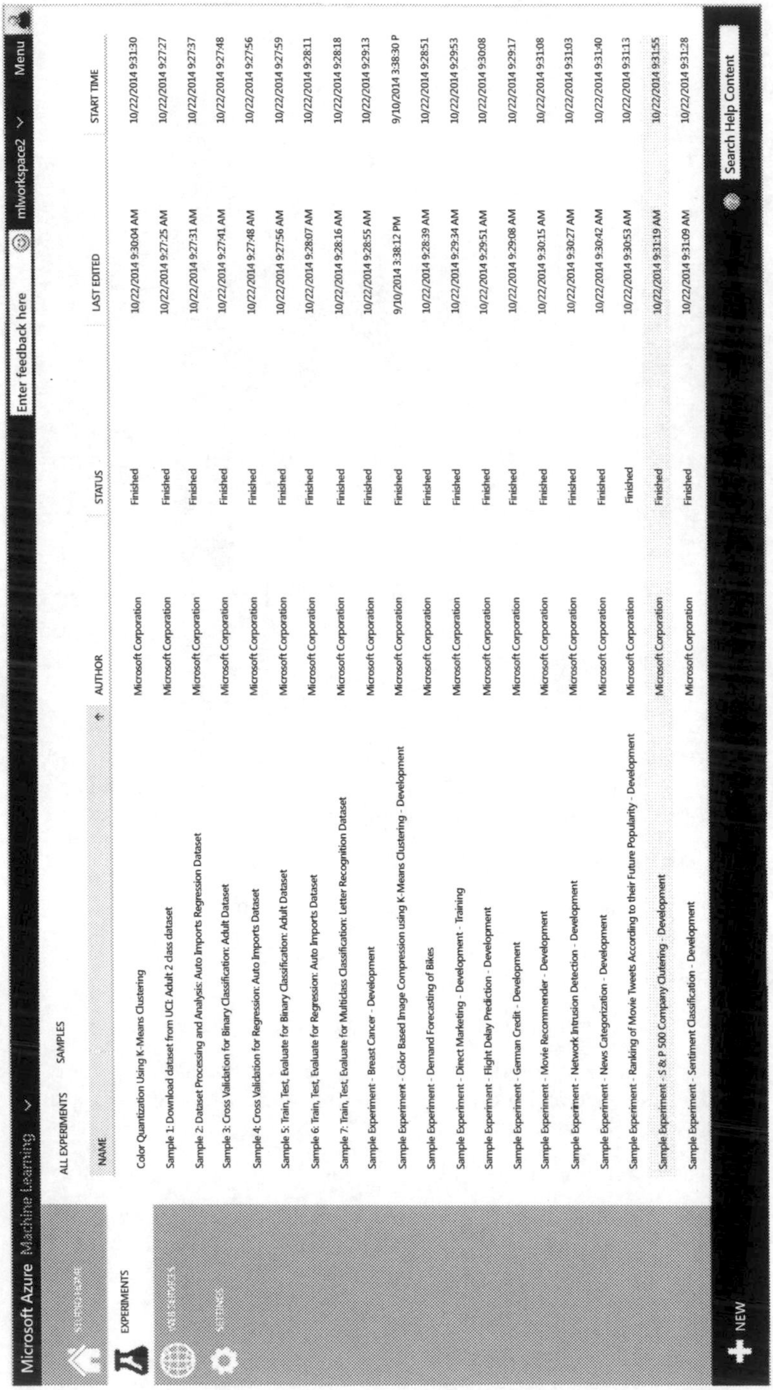

Figure 7-2. Experiment samples in ML Studio

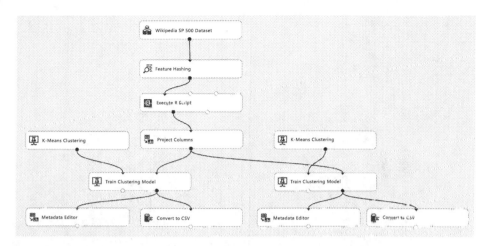

Figure 7-3. *Creating your first k-means clustering model in ML Studio*

Feature Hashing

In machine learning, the input feature(s) can be free text. A common approach to representing free text is to use a bag of words. Each word is represented as a token. Every time the word appears in the text, a 1 is assigned to the token. And if the word does not appear, a 0 is assigned.

However, the bag of words model will not scale because the number of possible words is not known beforehand. Imagine representing a token for every word in the descriptive text of each S&P 500 company. The dimensionality of the inputs can be potentially large. Hence, a common approach is to use a hash function to transform all the tokens into numerical features, and restrict the range of possible hash values. To do this, feature hashing (also known as the "hashing trick") is commonly used in machine learning communities to prepare the dataset before it is used as input for machine learning algorithms.

In this example, the **Feature Hashing** module is used to perform hashing on the descriptive text of the S&P 500 companies. Underneath the hood, the Feature Hashing module uses the Vowpal Wabbit library to perform 32-bit murmurhash hashing. For this exercise, the hashing bit size is set to **12**, and **N-grams**. After the Feature Hashing module has executed, you will see that the descriptive text has been converted into a large number of columns, with column names prefixed with Text_HashingFeature_ (shown in Figure 7-4).

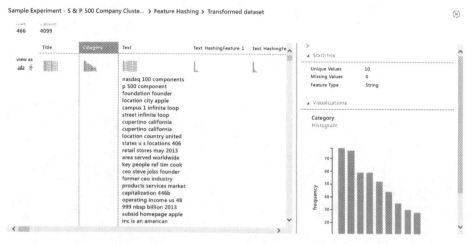

Figure 7-4. *Feature hashing*

■ **Note** The Vowpal Wabbit library is an open source machine learning library.
See `https://github.com/JohnLangford/vowpal_wabbit/wiki/Tutorial` for more information.

MurmurHash is a family of non-cryptographic hash functions that provide a good distribution,
avalanche behavior, and collision resistance. See `https://code.google.com/p/smhasher/`
for more information on the MurmurHash family of hash functions.

Identifying the Right Features

When using a k-means cluster for customer segmentation, you will need to identify the
features that will be used during the clustering process. After feature hashing has been
performed, a large number of features will have been computed based on the descriptive text.

Principal Components Analysis (PCA) is a powerful statistical technique that can
be used for identifying a smaller number of features (i.e. principal components) that
captures the key essence of the original features.

In this sample experiment, you will learn how to perform principal component
analysis using R. Specifically, you will be using the **Execute R Script** module to execute
the following R script (which has been provided as part of the sample experiment).

```
# Map 1-based optional input ports to variables
dataset1 <- maml.mapInputPort(1) # class: data.frame

# Sample operation
titles_categories = dataset1[,1:2]
pca = prcomp(dataset1[,4:4099])
top_pca_scores = data.frame(pca$x[,1:10])
data.set = cbind(titles_categories,top_pca_scores)
```

```
# You'll see this output in the R Device port.
# It'll have your stdout, stderr and PNG graphics device(s).
plot(pca)

# Select data.frame to be sent to the output Dataset port
maml.mapOutputPort("data.set");
```

From the R script, you will notice that the R function prcomp is used. The input to prcomp includes column 4 to 4099 of dataset1. The computed results are stored in the variable pca. For this sample experiment, you obtain the top 10 principal components, and use these as inputs to the k-means clustering algorithm.

After you have run the experiment, you can click on the **Execute R Script** module, and choose to visualize the result dataset. Figure 7-5 shows the result dataset, and the top 10 principal components (PC) that are computed.

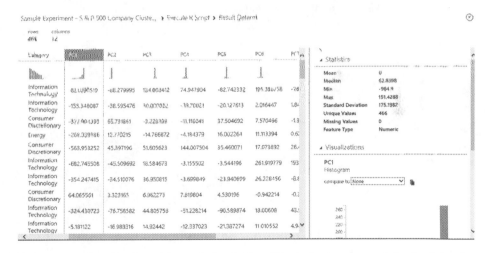

Figure 7-5. *Visualization of the result dataset (top 10 principal components for the dataset)*

■ **Note**   Refer to http://en.wikipedia.org/wiki/Principal_component_analysis to learn more about PCA.

In R, there are several functions that can be used for performing PCA. These include pca( ), prcomp( ), and princomp( ). prcomp( ) is commonly used because it is numerically more stable, and returns an R object with the following information: eigenvectors, square root of the eigenvalues, and scores.

See Chapter 3 for learning more on how you can use R with Azure Machine Learning.

Properties of K-Means Clustering

From Figure 7-3, you will see that k-means clustering is used twice in the experiment. The main difference between the two k-means clustering modules is the number of centroids (i.e. value of k). This is also the same as the number of segments or clusters you want from the k-means algorithm. For the left k-means clustering, the sample experiment has specified that the value of k to be 3 (i.e. the k-means clustering model will identify 3 clusters); whereas the right k-means clustering model specified the value of k to be 4.

You can see the number of centroids specified by clicking on each of the k-means clustering rectangles. Figure 7-6 shows the various properties of the K-Means clustering model, which include

- Number of centroids
- Metric: Metric is used to compute the distance between clusters
- Initialization: The method use to specify the seed the initial centroids
- Iterations: The number of iterations used

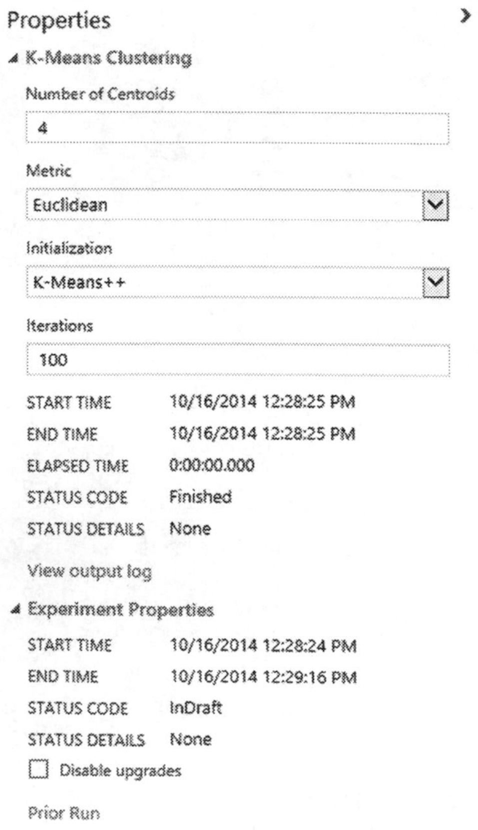

Properties   ❯

◢ K-Means Clustering

Number of Centroids

| 4 |

Metric

| Euclidean ▼ |

Initialization

| K-Means++ ▼ |

Iterations

| 100 |

START TIME	10/16/2014 12:28:25 PM
END TIME	10/16/2014 12:28:25 PM
ELAPSED TIME	0:00:00.000
STATUS CODE	Finished
STATUS DETAILS	None

View output log

◢ Experiment Properties

START TIME	10/16/2014 12:28:24 PM
END TIME	10/16/2014 12:29:16 PM
STATUS CODE	InDraft
STATUS DETAILS	None

☐ Disable upgrades

Prior Run

Figure 7-6. *Properties of the k-means clustering model*

When performing clustering, the user will need to specify the distance measure between any two points in the space. In ML Studio, this is defined by the Metric property. Two distance measures are supported: Euclidean (also known as L2 norm) and cosine distance. Depending on the characteristics of the input data and the use case, the user should select the relevant Metric property used by k-means clustering.

■ **Note** When performing clustering, it is important to be able to measure the distance (or similarity) between points and vectors. The Euclidean and cosine distances are common distance measures that are used.

Euclidean distance: Given two points, p1 and p2, the Euclidean distance between p1 and p2 is the length of the line segment that connects the two points. The Euclidean distance can also be used to measure the distance between two vectors.

Cosine distance: Given two vectors v1 and v2, the cosine distance is the cosine of the angle between v1 and v2.

The choice of the distance measure to use is often domain-specific.

Euclidean distance is sensitive to the scale/magnitude of the vectors that are compared. It is important to note that even though two vectors can be relatively similar, but if the scale of the features are significantly different, the Euclidean distance might show that the two vectors are different. In such cases, cosine distance is often used, since regardless of the scale, the cosine angle between the two vectors would have been small.

After selecting the metric for the distance measure, you will need to choose the centroid initialization algorithm. In Azure Machine Learning, this is defined by the Initialization property. Five centroid initialization algorithms are supported. Table 7-1 shows the different centroid initialization algorithms.

Table 7-1. K-means Cluster, Centroid Initialization Algorithms

Centroid Initialization Algorithm	Description
Default	Picks first N points as initial centroids
Random	Picks initial centroids randomly
K-Means++	K-means++ centroid initialization
K-Means+ Fast	K-means++ centroid initialization with P:=1 (where the farthest centroid is picked in each iteration of the algorithm)
Evenly	Picks N points evenly as initial centroids

These properties have already been pre-configured for you in the sample experiments.

At this point, you are ready to run the experiment. Click **Run** on the bottom panel of ML Studio. Once the experiment has successfully executed, two sets of clusters have been produced. The **Metadata Editor** module is used to change the metadata associated with columns in the dataset to include the assigned cluster. In addition, the **Convert to CSV** module is used to convert the results to comma-separate values, which allows you to download the result set.

Congratulations! You have successfully run your first company segmentation experiment using the **K-Means Clustering** module in ML Studio.

Customer Segmentation of Wholesale Customers

From the earlier section, you learned the key modules used in the sample experiment (K-Means Clustering, Train Clustering Model) to perform customer segmentation.

In this section, you will learn step-by-step how to build the clustering model to perform customer segmentation for a wholesale customer dataset.

■ **Note** The wholesale customers dataset is available on the UCI Machine Learning Repository. The dataset contains eight columns (referred to as attributes or features) and contains information on the customers of a wholesale distributor, operating in different regions.

The columns include annual spending on fresh milk, grocery, frozen, detergents, paper, and delicatessen products. In addition, it also includes information on the channel of the customer (hotel/café/restaurant) or retail.

Refer to http://archive.ics.uci.edu/ml/datasets/Wholesale+customers.

Loading the Data from the UCI Machine Learning Repository

Let's get started by using a Reader module to retrieve the data from the UCI Machine Repository. To do this, drag and drop a **Reader** module (Data Input and Output) from the toolbox. Next, configure the Reader module to read from the Http source, and provide the URL for the dataset: http://archive.ics.uci.edu/ml/machine-learning-databases/00292/Wholesale%20customers%20data.csv

Figure 7-7. shows the Reader module and its configuration.

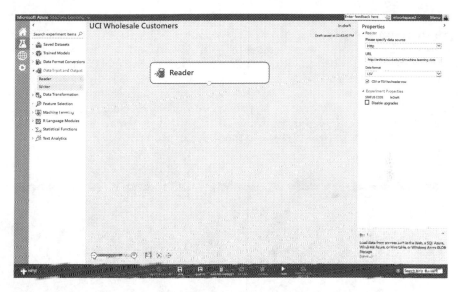

Figure 7-7. *Using the Reader module to read data from a HTTP data source*

Using K-Means Clustering for Wholesale Customer Segmentation

For this experiment, you will use all eight columns from the dataset as inputs for performing clustering. To do this, drag and drop the **K-Means Clustering** and **Train Clustering Model**, and connect the modules together based on what is shown in Figure 7-8.

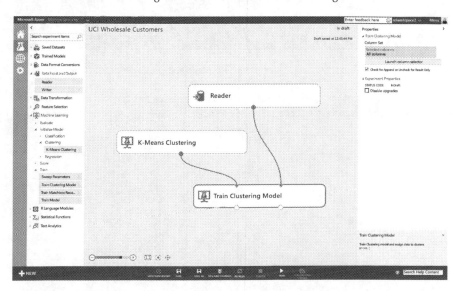

Figure 7-8. *Using K-Means Clustering and the Train Clustering model*

To configure each of the modules, click on the module, and specify the values using the **Properties** pane on the right side of the screen. For the K-Means Clustering module, configure it to identify four clusters (**Number of Centroids = 4**), and use the **Euclidean** distance measure. Use the default 100 number of iterations. For the Train Clustering Mode module, configure it to use **all** the features when performing clustering.

Finally, you will want to visualize the results after the experiment has run successfully. To do this, you will use the **Metadata Editor** module. Configure the Metadata Editor such that it uses **all** the features that are produced by the **Train Clustering Model** module. Figure 7-9. shows the final design of the clustering experiment.

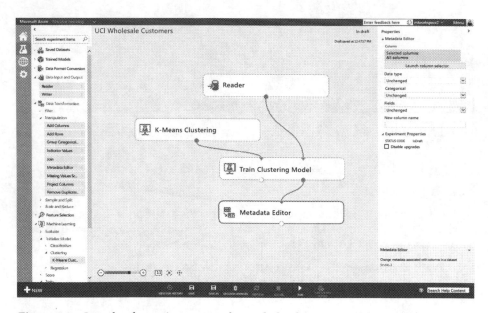

Figure 7-9. *Completed experiment to perform wholesale customer segmentation*

After the experiment has successfully run, you will be able to right-click the **Results** dataset output of the **Metadata Editor** module to see the cluster assignment (shown in Figure 7-10).

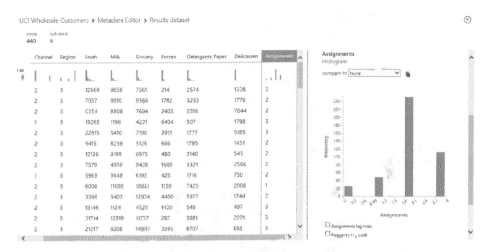

Figure 7-10. *Histogram showing cluster assignments for wholesale customers*

Cluster Assignment for New Data

What happens if you have new customers, and you want to assign them to one of the clusters that you identified? In this section, you will learn how to use the **Assign to Cluster** module.

In this example, you will first split the input dataset into two sets. The first set will be used for training the clustering model, and the second set will be used for cluster assignments. For practical use cases, the second dataset will be new data that you have newly acquired (e.g. new customers whom you want to assign to a cluster). To split the input dataset, you will use the **Split** module (in **Data Transformation ➤ Sample and Split**), and configure it such that it redirects 90% of the input data to its first output, and the remaining 10% to the second output. You will use the data from the first output of the Split module to train the clustering model.

Figure 7-11 shows the modified clustering experiment design where you added the Assign to Cluster and Split modules. To configure the Assign to Cluster module, click the module, and click the **Launch** column selector to select all columns. **Link** the output of the Assign to Cluster module to the Metadata Editor module. When a new observations is made, it is assigned to the cluster whose centroid has the closest distance.

You are now ready to run the experiment to perform cluster assignment. After the experiment has run successfully, you can visualize the results by right-clicking the **Results** dataset of the Metadata Editor module, and choosing **Visualize**.

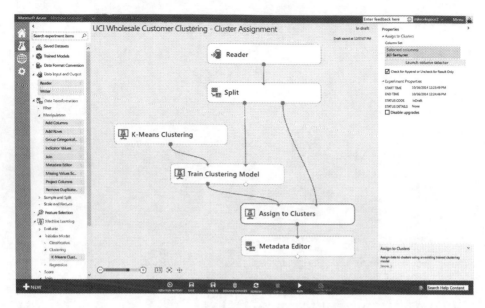

Figure 7-11. *Experiment to perform cluster assignment using the trained clustering model*

Congratulations! You have successfully built a k-means clustering model, and used the trained model for assigning new data to clusters.

Summary

In this chapter, you learned how to create a k-means clustering model using Azure Machine Learning. To jumpstart the learning, you used the sample experiment that is available in Azure Machine Learning, which performs segmentation of S&P 500 companies (based on each companies' descriptive text). You learned about the key modules that are available in ML Studio for performing clustering: K-Means Clustering and the Train Clustering Model. You learned how to use feature hashing to vectorize the input (which consists of free text), and PCA to identify the principal components.

In addition, you learned the steps to perform k-means clustering on a wholesale customer dataset, and how to use the trained model to perform cluster assignments for new data.

CHAPTER 8

■ ■ ■

Building Predictive Maintenance Models

The leading manufacturers are now investing in predictive maintenance, which holds the potential to reduce cost yet increase margin and customer satisfaction. Though traditional techniques such as statistics and manufacturing have helped, the industry is still plagued by serious quality issues and the high cost of business disruption when components fail. Advances in machine learning offer a unique opportunity to improve customer satisfaction and reduce service downtime. This chapter shows how to build models for predictive maintenance using Microsoft Azure Machine Learning. Through examples we will demonstrate how you can use Microsoft Azure Machine Learning to build, validate, and deploy a predictive model for predictive maintenance.

Overview

According to Ahmet Duyar, an expert in fault detection and former Visiting Researcher at NASA, a key cause of reduced productivity in the manufacturing industry is low asset effectiveness that results from equipment breakdowns and unnecessary maintenance interventions. In the US alone, the cost of excess maintenance and lost productivity is estimated at $740B, so we clearly need better approaches to maintenance (Duyar, 2011).

Predictive maintenance techniques are designed to predict when maintenance should be performed on a piece of equipment even before it breaks down. By accurately predicting the failure of a component you can reduce unplanned downtime and extend the lifetime of your equipment. Predictive maintenance also offers cost savings since it increases the efficiency of repairs: an engineer can target repair work to the predicted failure and complete the work faster as a result. They don't need to spend too much time trying to find the cause of the equipment failure. With predictive maintenance, plant operators can be more proactive and fix issues even before their equipment breaks down.

It is worth clarifying the difference between predictive and preventive maintenance since the two are often confused. Preventive maintenance refers to scheduled maintenance that is typically planned in advance. While useful and in many cases necessary, preventive maintenance can be expensive and ineffective at catching issues that develop in between scheduled appointments. In contrast, predictive maintenance aims to predict failures before they happen.

Let's use car servicing as an example to illustrate the difference. When you buy a car, the dealer typically recommends regular services based on time or mileage. For instance some car manufacturers recommend a full service after 6,000 and 10,000 miles. This is a good example of preventive maintenance. As you approach 6,000 miles, your dealer will send a reminder for you to schedule your full service. In contrast, through predictive maintenance, many car manufacturers would prefer to monitor the performance of your car on an ongoing basis through data relayed by sensors from your car to a database system. With this data, they can detect when your transmission or timing belt are beginning to show signs of impending failure and will call you for maintenance, regardless of your car's mileage.

Predictive maintenance is a form of non-destructive monitoring that occurs during the normal operation of the equipment. Sensors installed on the equipment collect valuable data that can be used to predict and prevent failures.

Current techniques for predictive maintenance include vibration analysis, acoustical analysis, infrared monitoring, oil analysis, and model-based condition modeling. Vibration analysis uses sensors such as accelerometers installed on a motor to determine when it is operating abnormally. According to Ahmet Duyar, vibration analysis is the most widely used approach to condition monitoring, accounting for up 85% of all systems sold. Acoustical analysis uses sonic or ultrasound analysis to detect abnormal friction and stress in rotating machines. While sonic techniques can detect problems in mechanical machines, ultrasound is more flexible and can detect issues in both mechanical and electrical machines. Infrared analysis has the widest range of applications, spanning low- to high-speed equipment and also mechanical and electrical devices.

Model-based condition monitoring uses mathematical models to predict failures. First developed by NASA, this technique has a learning phase in which it learns the characteristics of normal operating conditions. On completion of the learning phase, the system enters the production phase where it monitors the equipment's condition. It compares the performance of the equipment to the data collected in the learning phase, and will flag an issue if it detects a serious deviation from the normal operation of the machine. This is a form of anomaly detection where the monitoring system flags an issue when the machine deviates significantly from normal operating conditions.

▓ **Note**   Refer to the following resources for more details on predictive maintenance:

http://en.wikipedia.org/wiki/Predictive_maintenance and

Ahmet Duyar, "Simplifying predictive maintenance", Orbit Vol. 31 No.1, pp. 38-45, 2011.

The Business Problem

Imagine that you are a data scientist at a semiconductor manufacturer. Your employer wants you to do the following:

- Build a model that predicts yield failure on their manufacturing process, and

- Through your analysis provide the factors that lead to yield failures in their process.

This is a very important business problem for semiconductor manufacturers since their process can be complex and involves several stages from raw sand to the final integrated circuits. Given the complexity, there are several factors that can lead to yield failures downstream in the manufacturing process. Identifying the most important factors will help process engineers to improve the yield and reduce error rates and cost of production, leading to increased productivity.

■ **Note** You will need to have an account on Azure Machine Learning. Please refer to Chapter 2 for instructions to set up your new account if you do not have one yet.

In Chapter 1, you saw that the data science process typically follows these five steps.

1. Define the business problem
2. Data acquisition and preparation
3. Model development
4. Model deployment
5. Monitoring model performance

Having defined the business problem, you will explore data acquisition and preparation, model development, evaluation, and deployment in the remainder of this chapter.

Data Acquisition and Preparation

Let's explore how to load data from source systems and analyze the data in Azure Machine Learning.

The Dataset

For this exercise, you will use the SECOM dataset from the University of California at Irvine's machine learning database. This dataset from the semiconductor manufacturing industry was provided by Michael McCann and Adrian Johnston.

145

■ **Note**   The SECOM data set is available at the University of California at Irvine's Machine Learning Repository. The dataset contains 1,567 examples, each with 591 features. Of the 1567 examples, 104 of them represent yield failures.

The features or columns represent sensor readings from 590 points in the manufacturing process. In addition, it also includes a timestamp and the yield result (i.e. a simple pass or fail) for each example.

Refer to http://archive.ics.uci.edu/ml/machine-learning-databases/secom/.

Data Loading

Azure Machine Learning enables you to load data from several sources including your local machine, the Web, SQL Database on Azure, Hive tables, or Azure Blob storage.

Loading Data from Your Local File System

The easiest way to load data is from your local machine. You can do this through the following steps.

1. Point your browser to https://studio.azureml.net and log into your workspace in Azure Machine Learning.

2. Next, click the **Experiments** item from the menu on the left pane.

3. Click the **+New** button at the bottom left side of the window, and then select **Dataset** from the new menu shown in Figure 8-1.

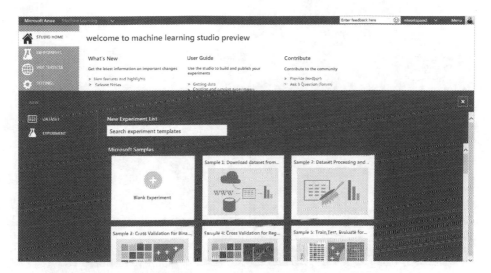

Figure 8-1. *Loading a new dataset from your local machine*

4. When you choose the option **From Local File** you will be prompted to select the data file to load from your machine.

Loading Data from Other Sources

You can load data from non-local sources using the **Reader** module in Azure Machine Learning. Specifically, with the **Reader** module you can load data from the Web, SQL Database on Azure, Azure Table, Azure Blob storage, or Hive tables. To do this you will have to create a new experiment before calling the **Reader** module. Use the following steps to load data from any of the above sources with the **Reader** module.

1. Point your browser to `https://studio.azureml.net` and log into your workspace in Azure Machine Learning.

2. Next, click the **Experiments** item from the menu on the left pane.

3. Click the **+New** button at the bottom left side of the window, and then select **Experiment** from the new menu. A new experiment is launched with a blank canvas, as shown in Figure 8-2.

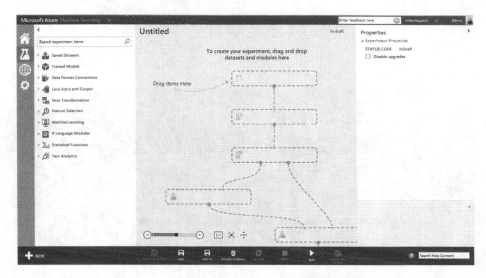

Figure 8-2. Starting a new experiment in Azure Machine Learning

4. Open the menu item **Data Input and Output** and you will see two modules, **Reader** and **Writer**.

5. Drag the **Reader** module from the menu to any position on the canvas.

6. Click the **Reader** module in the canvas and its properties will be shown on the right pane under **Reader**. Now specify the data source in the drop-down menu and then enter the values of all required parameters. The Account Name and Account Key refer to a storage account on Microsoft Azure. You can obtain these parameters from the Azure portal as follows:

   a. Log in to Microsoft Azure at http://azure.microsoft.com.

   b. On the top menu, click **Portal**. This takes you to the Azure portal.

   c. Select **storage** from the menu on the left pane. This lists all your storage accounts in the right pane.

   d. Click the storage account that contains the data you need for your machine learning model.

   e. At the bottom of the screen, click the key icon labeled **Manage Access Keys**. Your storage account name and access keys will be displayed. Use the **Primary Access Key** as your Account Key in the **Reader** module in Azure Machine Learning.

▓ **Note** You can load several datasets from multiple sources into Azure Machine Learning using the above instructions. Note, however, that each **Reader** module only loads a single dataset at a time.

For this project, import the two SECOM datasets from the UCI Machine Learning database and join them into a new file stored locally. The first dataset only has the sensor readings, while the second dataset has the labels (i.e. the yield data). Then load the joined dataset into Azure Machine Learning using the first approach above.

Data Analysis

Figure 8-3 shows the first part of the experiment that covers data preparation. The data is loaded and preprocessed for missing values using the **Missing Values Scrubber** module. Following this, summary statistics are obtained and the **Filter Based Feature Selection** module is used to determine the most important variables for prediction.

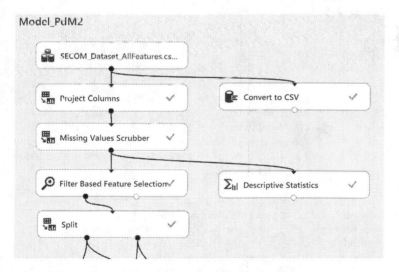

Figure 8-3. *Preprocessing the SECOM dataset*

Figure 8-4 shows a snapshot of the SECOM data as seen in Azure Machine Learning. As you can see, there are 1,567 rows and 592 columns in the dataset. In addition, Azure Machine Learning also shows the number of unique values per feature and the number of missing values. You can see that many of the sensors have missing values. Further, some of the sensors have a constant reading for all rows. For example, sensor #6 has a reading of 100 for all rows. Such features will have to be eliminated as they add no value to the prediction since there is no variation in their readings.

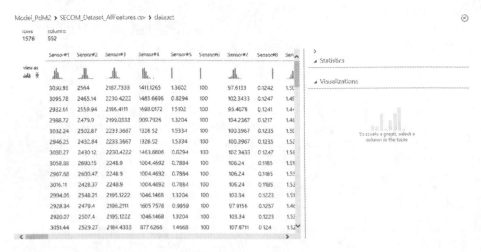

Figure 8-4. *Visualizing the SECOM dataset in Azure Machine Learning*

Feature Selection

Feature selection is critical in this case since it provides the answer to your second business problem. Indeed, with over 590 features, you must perform feature selection to identify the subset of features that are useful to build a good model and eliminate irrelevant and redundant features. With so many features, you risk the curse of dimensionality. If there are a large number of features, the learning problem can be difficult because the many "extra" features can confuse the learning algorithm and cause it to have high variance. It's also important to note that machine learning algorithms are very computationally intensive, and reducing the number of features can greatly reduce the time required and train the model, enabling the data scientist to perform experiments in less time. Through careful feature selection, you can find the most influential variables for the prediction. Let's see how to do feature selection in Azure Machine Learning.

To perform feature selection in Azure Machine Learning, drag the module named **Filter Based Feature Selection** from the list of modules in the left pane. You can find this module by either searching for it in the search box or by opening the **Feature Selection** category. To use this module, you need to connect it to a dataset as the input. Figure 8-5 shows how to use it to perform feature selection on the SECOM dataset. Before running the experiment, use the **Launch column selector** in the right pane to define the target variable for prediction. In this case, choose the column **Yield_Pass_Fail** as the target since this is what you wish to predict. When you are done, set the number of desired features to 100. This instructs the feature selector in Azure Machine Learning to find the top 100 variables.

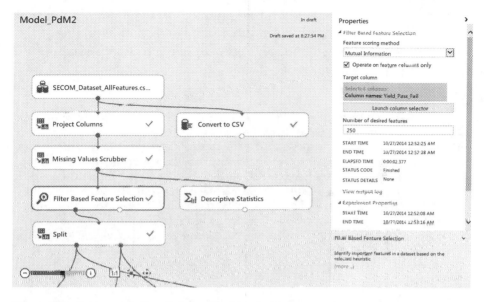

Figure 8-5. *Feature selection in Azure Machine Learning*

You also need to choose the scoring method that will be used for feature selection. Azure Machine Learning offers the following options for scoring:

- Pearson correlation

- Mutual information

- Kendall correlation

- Spearman correlation

- Chi Squared

- Fischer score

- Count-based

The correlation methods find the set of variables that are highly correlated with the output, but have low correlation among themselves. The correlation is calculated using Pearson, Kendall, or Spearman correlation coefficients, depending on the option you choose.

The Fisher score uses the Fisher criterion from statistics to rank variables. In contrast, the mutual information option is an information theoretic approach that uses mutual information to rank variables. The mutual information measures the dependence between the probability density of each variable and that of the outcome variable.

Finally, the Chi Squared option selects the best features using a test for independence; in other words, it tests whether each variable is independent of the outcome variable. It then ranks the variables using the Chi Squared test.

■ **Note** See http://en.wikipedia.org/wiki/Feature_selection#Correlation_
feature_selection or http://jmlr.org/papers/volume3/guyon03a/guyon03a.pdf
for more information on feature selection strategies.

When you run the experiment, the **Filter Based Feature Selection** module produces
two outputs: first, the filtered dataset lists the actual data for the most important
variables. Second, the module shows a list of the variables by importance with the scores
for each selected variable. Figure 8-6 shows the results of the features. In this case, you set
the number of features to 100 and you use mutual information for scoring and ranking
the variables. Figure 8-6 shows 101 columns since the results set includes the target
variable (i.e. Yield_Pass_Fail) plus the top 100 variables including sensor #60, sensor
#248, sensor #520, sensor #104, etc. The last row of the results shows the score for each
selected variable. Since the variables are ranked, the scores decrease from left to right.

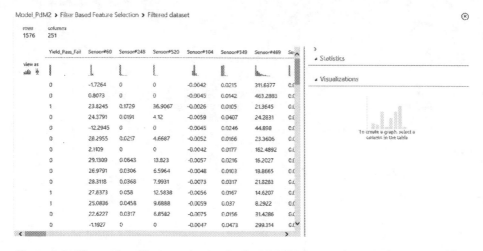

Figure 8-6. *The results of feature selection for the SECOM dataset showing the top variables*

Note that the selected variables will vary based on the scoring method, so it is worth
experimenting with different scoring methods before choosing the final set of variables.
The Chi Squared and mutual information scoring methods produce a similar ranking of
variables for the SECOM dataset.

Training the Model

Having completed the data preprocessing, the next step is to train the model to predict
the yield. Since the response variable is binary, you can treat this as a binary classification
problem. You can use any of the two-class classification algorithms in Azure Machine
Learning such as two-class logistic regression, two-class boosted decision trees, two-class
decision forest, two-class neural networks, etc.

■ **Note**   All predictive maintenance problems are not created equal. Some problems will require different techniques besides classification. For instance, if the goal is to determine **when** a part will fail, you will need to use survival analysis. Alternatively, if the goal is to predict energy consumption, you may use a forecasting technique or a regression method that predicts continuous outcomes. Hence you need to understand the business problem in order to find the most appropriate technique to use. One size does not fit all!

Figure 8-7 shows the full experiment to predict the yield from SECOM data. The top half of the experiment, up to the **Split** module, implements the data preprocessing phase. The **Split** module splits the data into two samples, a training sample comprising 70% of the initial dataset, and a test sample with the remaining 30%.

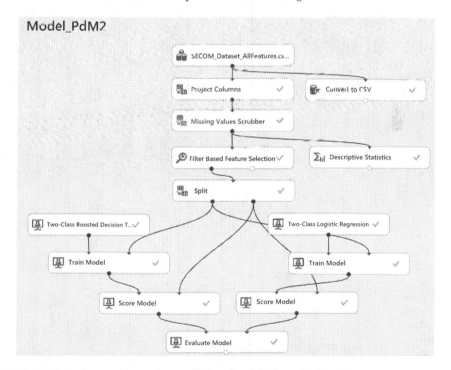

Figure 8-7. *An experiment for predicting the yield from SECOM data*

In this experiment, you compare two classification algorithms to find the best predictor of yield. The left branch after the **Split** module uses the two-class boosted decision tree, while the right branch uses the two-class logistic regression algorithm that is widely used in statistics. Each of these algorithms are trained with the same training sample and tested with the same test sample. You use the module named **Train Model** to train each algorithm, and the **Score Model** for testing. The module named **Evaluate Model** is used to evaluate the accuracy of these two classification models.

Model Testing and Validation

Once the model is trained, the next step is to test it with a hold-out sample to avoid over-fitting and evaluate model generalization. We have shown how we performed this using a 30% sample for testing the trained model. Another strategy to avoid over-fitting and evaluate model generalization is cross-validation, which was discussed in Chapter 6. By default, Azure Machine Learning uses 10-fold cross-validation. With this approach, you use 10 hold-out samples instead of one for testing. To perform cross-validation for this problem you can simply replace any pair of the **Train Model** and **Score Model** modules with the module named **Cross Validate Model**. Figure 8-8 shows how to perform cross-validation with the **Two-Class Logistic Regression** portion of this experiment. You will also need to use the whole dataset from the **Filter Based Feature Selection** as your input dataset. For cross-validation there is no need to split the data into training and test sets with the **Split** module since the module named **Cross Validate Model** will do the required data splits.

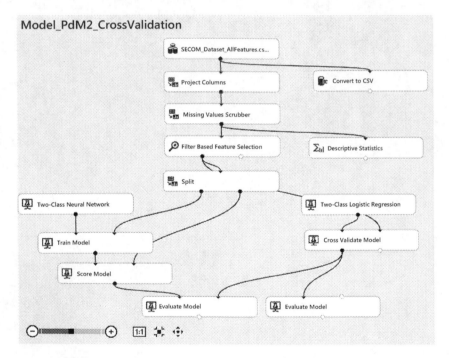

Figure 8-8. *A modified experiment with cross-validation*

Model Performance

The **Evaluate Model** module is used to measure the performance of a trained model. This module takes two datasets as inputs. The first is a scored dataset from a tested model. The second is an optional dataset for comparison. After running the experiment, you can check your model's performance by clicking the small circle at the bottom of the module named **Evaluate Model**. This module provides the following methods to measure the performance of a classification model such as the propensity model:

- The receiver operating characteristic, or ROC curve, which plots the rate of true positives to false positives

- The lift curve (also known as the gains curve), which plots the number of true positives vs. the positive rate

- Precision vs. recall chart

- Confusion matrix that shows type I and II errors

Figure 8-9 shows the ROC curve for the propensity model you built earlier. The ROC curve visually shows the performance of a predictive binary classification model. The diagonal line from (0,0) to (1,1) on the chart shows the performance of random guessing; so if you randomly selected the yield, your response would be on this diagonal line. A good predictive model should do much better than random guessing. Hence, on the ROC curve, a good model should lie above the diagonal line. The ideal or perfect model that is 100% accurate will have a vertical line from (0,0) to (0,1), followed by a horizontal line from (0,1) to (1,1).

Model_PdM2 ❯ Evaluate Model ❯ Evaluation results

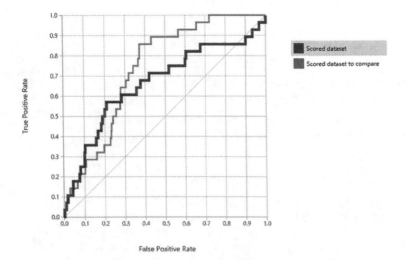

Figure 8-9. *Two ROC curves comparing the performance of logistic regression and boosted decision tree models for yield prediction*

One way to measure the performance from the ROC curve is to measure the area under the curve (AUC). The higher the area under the curve, the better the model's performance. The ideal model will have an AUC of 1.0, while random guessing will have an AUC of 0.5. The logistic regression model you built has an AUC of 0.667 while the boosted decision tree model has a slightly higher AUC of 0.741! In this experiment, the two-class boosted decision tree had the following parameters:

- Maximum number of leaves per tree = 50

- Maximum number of training instances required to form a leaf = 10

- Learning rate = 0.4

- Number of trees constructed = 1000

- Random number seed = 1

In addition, Azure Machine Learning also provides the confusion matrix as well as precision and recall rates for both models. By clicking each of the two curves, the tool shows the confusion matrix, precision, and recall rates for the select model. If you click the bottom curve or the legend named "scored dataset to compare," the tool shows the performance data for the logistic regression model.

Figure 8-10 shows the confusion matrix for the logistic regression model. The confusion matrix has the following four cells:

- **True positives**: These are cases where yield failed and the model correctly predicts this.

- **True negatives**: In the historical dataset, the yield passed, and the model correctly predicts a pass.

- **False positives**: In this case, the model incorrectly predicts that the yield would fail when in fact it was a pass. This is commonly referred to as Type I error. The boosted decision tree model you built had only two false positives.

- **False negatives**: Here the model incorrectly predicts that the yield would pass when in reality it failed. This is also known as Type II error. The boosted decision tree model had 27 false negatives.

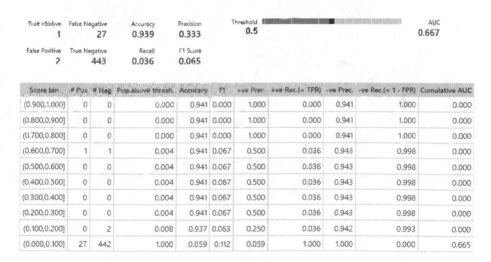

True Positive	False Negative	Accuracy	Precision		
1	27	0.939	0.333		
False Positive	True Negative	Recall	F1 Score		
2	443	0.036	0.065		

Threshold **▓▓▓▓▓▓▓▓▓▓▓▓▓▓▓▓▓▓** 0.5   AUC 0.667

Score bin	# Pos	# Neg	Pop.above thresh.	Accuracy	F1	+ve Prec.	+ve Rec.(= TPR)	-ve Prec.	-ve Rec.(= 1 - FPR)	Cumulative AUC
(0.900,1.000]	0	0	0.000	0.941	0.000	1.000	0.000	0.941	1.000	0.000
(0.800,0.900]	0	0	0.000	0.941	0.000	1.000	0.000	0.941	1.000	0.000
(0.700,0.800]	0	0	0.000	0.941	0.000	1.000	0.000	0.941	1.000	0.000
(0.600,0.700]	1	1	0.004	0.941	0.067	0.500	0.036	0.943	0.998	0.000
(0.500,0.600]	0	0	0.004	0.941	0.067	0.500	0.036	0.943	0.998	0.000
(0.400,0.500]	0	0	0.004	0.941	0.067	0.500	0.036	0.943	0.998	0.000
(0.300,0.400]	0	0	0.004	0.941	0.067	0.500	0.036	0.943	0.998	0.000
(0.200,0.300]	0	0	0.004	0.941	0.067	0.500	0.036	0.943	0.998	0.000
(0.100,0.200]	0	2	0.008	0.937	0.063	0.250	0.036	0.942	0.993	0.000
(0.000,0.100]	27	442	1.000	0.059	0.112	0.059	1.000	1.000	0.000	0.665

Figure 8-10. *Confusion matrix and more performance metrics*

In addition, Figure 8-10 shows the accuracy, precision, and recall of the model. Here are the formulas for these metrics:

Precision is the rate of true positives in the results.

$$Precision = \frac{tp}{tp+fp} = \frac{1}{1+2} = 0.333$$

Recall is the percentage of buyers that the model identifies and is measured as

$$Recall = \frac{tp}{tp+fn} = \frac{1}{1+443} = 0.036$$

Finally, the accuracy measures how well the model correctly identifies buyers and non-buyers, shown as

$$Accuracy = \frac{tp+tn}{tp+tn+fp+fn} = \frac{1+443}{1+443+2+27} = 0.939$$

where tp = true positive, tn = true negative, fp = false positive, and fn = false negative. The F1 score is a weighted average of precision and recall. In this case, it is quite low since the recall is very low.

Model Deployment

When you build and test a predictive model that meets your needs, you can use Azure Machine Learning to deploy it into production for business use. A key differentiator of Azure Machine Learning is the ease of deployment in production. Once a model is complete, it can be deployed very easily into production as a web service. Once deployed, the model can be invoked as a web service from multiple devices including servers, laptops, tablets, or even smart phones.

The following two steps are required to deploy a model into production.

1. Publish your experiment into the staging environment in Azure Machine Learning Studio.

2. From the Azure Management portal, move the experiment from the staging environment into production.

Let's review these steps in detail and see how they apply to your finished model built in the previous sections.

Publishing Your Model into Staging

To deploy your model into staging, follow these steps in Azure Machine Learning Studio.

1. Save your trained mode using the **Save As** button at the bottom of Azure Machine Learning Studio. Rename it to a new name of your choice.

    a. **Run** the experiment.

    b. Right-click the output of the training module (e.g. **Train Model**) and select the option **Save As Trained Model.**

    c. Delete any modules that were used for training (e.g. the **Split, Two-Class Boosted Decision Tree, Train Model, Evaluate Model**).

    d. Connect the newly saved model directly to the **Score Model** module.

    e. Re-run your experiment.

Before the deletion in Step 1c, your experiment should be as shown Figure 8-11.

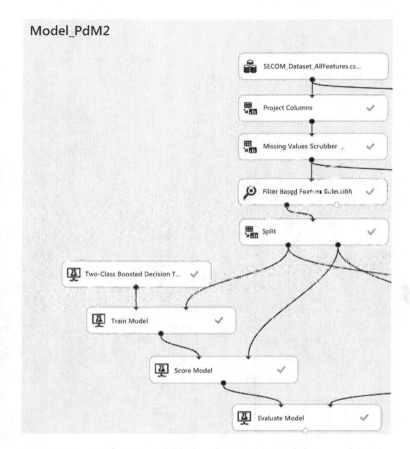

Figure 8-11. *Predictive model before the training modules were deleted*

After deleting the training modules and replacing them with the saved training model, the experiment should now appear as shown in Figure 8-12.

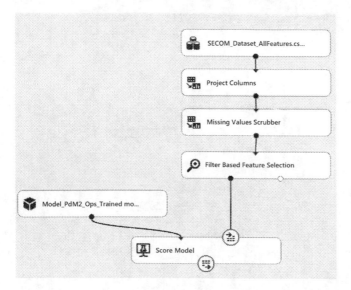

Figure 8-12. *The experiment that uses the saved training model*

2. Next, set your publishing input and output data ports.
    To do this,

    a. Right-click the right input port of the module named
        Score Model. Select the option **Set As Publish Input**.

    b. Right-click the output port of the **Score Model** module
        and select **Set As Publish Output**.

After these two steps, you will see two circles highlighting the chosen publish input
and output on the Score Model module. This is shown in Figure 8-12.

3. Once you assign the publish input and output ports, run
    the experiment and then publish it into staging by clicking
    Publish Web Service at the bottom of the screen.

Moving Your Model from Staging into Production

At this point your model is now in the staging environment, but is not yet running
in production. To publish it into production, you need to move it from the staging
environment to the production environment through the following steps.

1. Configure your new web service in Azure Machine Learning
    Studio and make it ready for production as follows:

    a. In Azure Machine Learning Studio, click the menu called
        Web Services on the right pane. It will show a list of all
        your web services.

    b.   Click the name of the new service you just created. Test it by clicking the **Test** URL.

    c.   Click the configuration tab, and then select yes for the option **Ready For Production?** Click the **Save** button at the bottom of the window. Now your model is ready to be published in production.

2.   Now switch to Azure Management Portal and publish your web service into production as follows:

    a.   Select **Machine Learning** on the right-hand pane in Azure Management Portal.

    b.   Choose the workspace with the experiment you want to deploy in production.

    c.   Click the name of your workspace, and then click the tab named **Web Services.**

    d.   Choose the **+Add** button at the bottom of the Azure Management Portal window.

Congratulations, you have just published your machine learning model into production. If you click your model from the **Web Services** tab, you will see details such as the number of predictions made by your model over a seven-day window. The service also shows the APIs you can use to call your model as a web service either in a request/response or batch execution mode. In addition, you also get sample code you can use to invoke your new web service in C#, Python, or R.

Summary

You began this chapter by exploring predictive maintenance, which shows the business opportunity and the promise of machine learning. Using the SECOM semiconductor manufacturing data from the University of California at Irvine's Machine Learning Data Repository, you learned how to build and deploy a predictive maintenance solution in Azure Machine Learning. In this step-by-step guide, we explained how to perform data preprocessing and analysis, which are critical for understanding the data. With that understanding of the data, you used a two-class logistic regression and a two-class boosted decision tree algorithm to perform classification. You also saw how to evaluate the performance of your models and avoid over-fitting. Finally, you saw how to deploy the finished model in production as a machine learning web service on Microsoft Azure.

Index

■ A

Analytics spectrum
    categories, 4
    data analysis, 5
    descriptive analysis, 5
    diagnostic analysis, 5
    predictive analysis, 5
    prescriptive analysis, 6
Area under curve (AUC), 103
Average computer
        memory price, 10
Azure machine learning, 156
    algorithms, 31–32
    automobile price data, 24
    building and testing, 21
    components, experiment, 22–23
    dataset, 25
    dataset visualization, 26
    deploying your model, 36–39
    features, 29–30
    iterative process, 22
    palette search, 25
    prediction, new data, 33–35
    preprocess, dataset, 26–28
    staging into production, 39–40
    visual workspace, 21
    web service, 40–42
    web service testing, 39
Azure Machine Learning, 88–89, 137

■ B

Bayes point machines (BPMs)
    average classifier, 78
    Azure Machine Learning, 79
    linear classifiers, 78
    training iterations, 79
BikeBuyer.csv file, 90

■ C

Churn models
    Azure Machine Learning
        Studio, 107–108
    consumer business, 107
    customer (*see* Customer churn model)
    effective strategy, 107
    training and testing, 108
Classification and Regression
        Tree (CART), 73
Customer churn model
    boosted decision tree and forest
        algorithms, 121
    classification algorithms, 109, 121
    confusion matrix, accuracy, precision,
        recall and F1 scores, 125, 127
    data preprocessing and selection
        feature selection modules, 114
        Metadata Editor, 119–121
        missing values scrubber, 117–119
        project columns, 115–116
        quantize properties, 118
        select columns, 116–117
        training data and label, 120
    decision tree, 121
    preparing and understanding data
        descriptive statistics, 113–114
        KDD Cup web site, 110
        machine learning model, 113
        Machine Learning Studio, 110
        Orange training and labels, 111, 113
        uploading dataset, 110–111
    ROC curve, 125–126
    Score and Evaluate model, 125
    Split module, properties, 122
    train model, 124
    two-class boosted decision tree
        and forest, 123–124

Customer propensity models
    Bike Buyer dataset, 91
    box-and-whisker icon, 94
    classification algorithm, 99
    confusion matrix, 103
    customer targeting models, 87
    data science process, 88
    demographic variables, 91
    histogram, 92
    IQR, 94
    logistic regression, 99
    log transformation, 93
    prediction error, 99
    predictive models, 105
    project columns, 100
    ROI, 87
    testing and validation, 101
    train module, 100
    true positives, 104
    visualizing data, 91
Customer segmentation models
    companies, 129
    consumer credit score, 130
    data analysts, 129
    K-means clustering
        (*see* K-means clustering)
    learning techniques, 130
    telecommunication industry, 130
    wholesale customers
        (*see* Wholesale customers)

▓ **D**

Data analysis
    Azure machine learning, 151
    feature selection, 150
    filter based feature
        selection module, 152
    launch column selector, 150
    missing values scrubber module, 149
    SECOM dataset, 149–150, 152
Data format conversions, 95
Data loading
    labels, 149
    local file system, 146–147
    local machine, 88–89
    non-local sources, 89–90, 147–148
Data mining technologies, 8
Data science
    academic disciplines, 4
    acquiring and data preparation, 11–12

    algorithms, 14
    analytics spectrum
        (*see* analytics spectrum)
    classification algorithms, 14
    clustering, 15–16
    competitive asset, 7
    content analysis, 17
    customer demand, 8
    definition, 11
    digital data, 8
    model development and
        deployment, 12
    model's performance, 12
    powerful processes, 3
    practitioners, 4
    processing power, 9
    recommendation engines, 18
Dataset, 145
Data transformation item, 95
Decision tree algorithms
    bagging and boosting, 74
    CART algorithm, 73
    data selection, 74
    Gini impurity, 73
    ID3, 73
    root nodes, 72
    training, 74

▓ **E**

Ensemble models
    algorithms, 18
    applications, 18–19
    building, 19
Evaluate model module, 155–157

▓ **F, G, H**

Feature selection, 96, 98
Filter based feature selection, 154
Fisher score, 151

▓ **I, J**

Iterative Dichotomizer 3 (ID3), 73

▓ **K**

K-means clustering
    categories, 130
    experiment samples, 132

feature hashing, 133
properties, 136, 137–138
right features, 134–135
segmentation of companies, 130

▓ L

Learning algorithms
   agglomerative and division, 79
   BPMs, 78–79
   centroid initialization methods, 82
   density-based algorithms, 80
   K-means clustering, 80–81
   mapping, 75
   partitioning-based clustering, 80
   regression algorithms
      (see Regression algorithms)
   supervised learning, 74
   SVMs, 76–78
   telecommunication, 75
Linear correlation module, 96

▓ M

maml.mapInputPort(1) method, 48
Metadata Editor module, 138
Missing values scrubber
      properties, 28–29

▓ N, O

Neural networks
   ART, 70
   hidden nodes, 71
   input and output nodes, 70
   propagations, 70
   rate of convergence, 71
   self-organizing maps, 70
   sigmoidal activate function, 70

▓ P, Q

PCA. See Principal Component
      Analysis (PCA)
Predictive maintenance models
   business problem, 145
   components, 143
   deployment, 158
   manufacturing industry, 143
   model-based condition, 144

repairs, 143
staging, 158–160
testing and validation, 154
training, 152–153
transmission, 144
vibration analysis, 144
Principal Components
      Analysis (PCA), 50, 52–53, 134
Project Columns properties, 27

▓ R

Receiver Operating
      Curve (ROC curve), 125, 155–126
Regression algorithms
   decision tree algorithms, 72–74
   linear regression, 68–69
   neural networks, 70–71
   numerical outcomes, 67
Regression model experiment, 35
Regression techniques, 16–17
ROC curve. See Receiver Operating
      Curve (ROC curve)
R, statistical programming language
   actuarial sciences, 43
   Azure Machine Learning, 44–45, 64
   bioinformatics, 43
   building and deploying
      Execute R Script module, 46–48
      language modules, 45
      maml.mapInputPort(1)
         method, 48
      ML Studio, 47–48
      visualization, 48, 50
   data preprocessing
      components, 53–54
      Execute R Script module, 51–52
      machine learning algorithm, 50
      Metadata Editor module, 51
      missing values scrubber
         module, 51
      PCA, 50, 52–53
      sample and CRM dataset, 50
   decision tree
      Adult Census Income Binary
         Classification dataset, 59–61
      library(), 61
      ML Studio, 62
      rpart, 59, 64
      view output log, 62, 64

R, statistical programming language (*cont.*)
    finance and banking, 43
    script bundle (zip)
        Execute R Script module, 56, 58
        folder containing, 54–55
        package, 55
        uploading, dataset, 55–56
    telecommunication, 43

■ S

Score model module, 33
Simulation, 17
Split module, 153
Staging
    Azure machine learning studio, 158
    into production, 160–161
    publishing, 160
    training modules, 159
Support vector machines (SVMs)
    hyperplane, 76
    kernel-based learning, 76

random number seed, 78
telecommunication, 76

■ T

Two-class boosted decision
    tree module, 104

■ U, V

UCI Machine Repository, 138

■ W, X, Y, Z

Wholesale customers
    cluster assignment, 141–142
    clustering model, 138
    Euclidean distance, 140
    K-means clustering, 139
    Metadata Editor, 140
    train clustering model, 139
    UCI Machine Repository, 138

Get the eBook for only $10!

Now you can take the weightless companion with you anywhere, anytime. Your purchase of this book entitles you to 3 electronic versions for only $10.

This Apress title will prove so indispensible that you'll want to carry it with you everywhere, which is why we are offering the eBook in 3 formats for only $10 if you have already purchased the print book.

Convenient and fully searchable, the PDF version enables you to easily find and copy code—or perform examples by quickly toggling between instructions and applications. The MOBI format is ideal for your Kindle, while the ePUB can be utilized on a variety of mobile devices.

Go to www.apress.com/promo/tendollars to purchase your companion eBook.